Foundations

Basics of the Christian Faith for Youth

George B. Thompson, Jr.
Kel Groseclose

An official resource for The United Methodist Church prepared by the General Board of Discipleship through the Division of Church School Publications and published by Graded Press, a division of The United Methodist Publishing House, 201 Eighth Avenue, South, P.O. Box 801, Nashville, Tennessee 37202. Printed in the United States of America.

Scripture quotations in this publication, unless otherwise indicated, are from the Revised Standard Version of the Bible, copyrighted 1946, 1952, © 1971, 1973 by the Division of Christian Education of the National Council of Churches of Christ in the U.S.A., and used by permission.

For permission to reproduce any material in this publication, call 615-749-6421, or write to Graded Press, Syndication—Permissions Office, 201 Eighth Avenue, South, P.O. Box 801, Nashville, Tennessee 37202.

To order copies of this publication, call toll free: 1-800-672-1789. Call Monday–Friday, 7:30–5:00 Central time or 8:30–4:30 Pacific time. Use your Cokesbury account, American Express, Visa, Discover, or MasterCard.

Editorial Team
    Jack A. Keller, Jr., Editor
    William L. Hamer, Assistant Editor
    Janet K. Zimmerman, Secretary

Design Team
    Adolph C. Lavin, Design Director
    Susan J. Scruggs, Layout Designer

Administrative Staff
    Orion N. Hutchinson, Jr., Editor of
        Church School Publications
    Nellie M. Moser, Executive Editor of
        Youth-Adult Publications

ART AND PHOTO CREDITS:
Cover, Jim Whitmer, Bob Taylor; p. 1, Karen H. Muller; p. 2, COMSTOCK; p. 8, H. Armstrong Roberts; p. 13, Rollin Kocsis; p. 16, Jim Whitmer; p. 17, © 1960 United Feature Syndicate, Inc.; pp. 18, 20, Jim Whitmer; p. 25, Roger Neal; p. 31, Jack A. Keller, Sr.; page 34, Bob Taylor; pp. 36, 37, Bill Finney; p. 38, Ken Whitmire Associates; p. 44, Jim Padgett; p. 49, Bob Coyle; p. 51, COMSTOCK; pp. 52–53, Charles Shaw; p. 59, Jean-Claude Lejeune; p. 61, © 1967 United Feature Syndicate, Inc.; p. 64, COMSTOCK; p. 65, Ewing Galloway; p. 66 Bruce Thomas; page 67, Bruce Thomas, Robert Rattner; p. 72, Jack A. Keller, Sr.; p. 77, The World Christian Fellowship Window. Used by permission of the Upper Room; p. 78, Charles Shaw.

TABLE OF CONTENTS

Chapter 1

What Makes Jesus So Special?

CORNERSTONE

The *Incarnation* means that God entered the world and human life in a unique and decisive way in Jesus Christ.

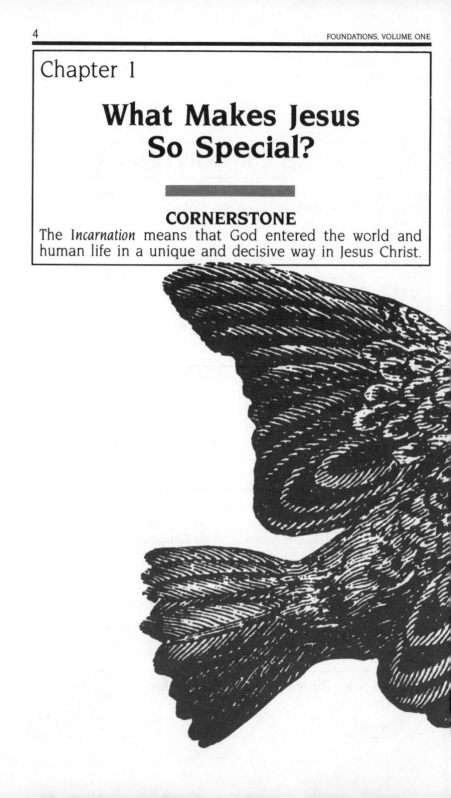

The Incarnation: Getting the Message Across

He knew his parents would be upset, but he didn't want to go to the Christmas Eve service. He was fifteen years old; he could think quite well for himself, thank you. And his head was filled with more questions about God and the church than answers. This business about God coming to earth in a baby born long ago in a no-account nation just didn't make sense to him.

Sure enough, his folks were none too pleased; but they went out alone into the cold December night to the midnight worship. Soon the sky darkened, and the wind built until it nearly screamed as it came around the corners of the house and tried to get through the door. The snow began to descend, first with a few gentle flakes, then followed immediately by a blizzard of white.

He heard a thumping at the window but saw nothing. Again came the sounds of bumping against the window. He ventured into the storm in time to see a small flock of birds seeking shelter from the icy blast. Unable to find refuge, they were banging against the glass. Just a few yards from the house was the garage. He tried to coax them there, but it was to no avail. He got a flashlight, opened the garage door wide, and showed them the way. They would not follow. He got parakeet food and scattered it along the path and put some on the garage floor. Still the birds thumped against the window pane.

If only I could become a bird for a few moments, he thought. *They would trust me and I could lead them all to safety.* At that moment the church bells began to chime out the joyful news of the Savior's birth. "Now I understand," he said as the snowflakes swirled around his head. "Now I understand why you had to do it. Thank you, God."

The God Who Is Down-to-Earth

The Incarnation is proof indeed that God is not remote and unfeeling. Ours is a "hands on" God who is always with us. God desires that his people know, love, and respect him. He had given the law through Moses. He had offered guidance through the forceful preaching of prophets. Now he would risk everything. He would send his son. Jesus told a parable of the wicked tenants (Luke 20:9-18) in which the owner tried various ways to gain the tenants' respect. Each time the owner failed. The owner of the vineyard said, "What shall I do? I will send my beloved son; it may be they will respect him" (Luke 20:13).

And so the eternal Word of God "became flesh and dwelt among us" (John 1:14). God wrapped up love and grace in a person, Jesus of Nazareth. God loved the world so much that he sent the very best—himself. It was a risky venture, but in the mind of God the possibilities far outweighed the dangers.

Given the angry response of some people and the total indifference of others, it's a wonder that God didn't take it all back. But the Incarnation is for all time, a gift forever to the whole world. This gift is available for you this very day. Because God found such a creative, imaginative way to show love, we are able to give ourselves wholly to love. Because God completely identified with us, we have the capacity to be compassionate.

God's love is vulnerable, available, accessible. God does not work by remote control. There are no lead shields, thick gloves, or robotic arms. The Incarnation tells us that a very down-to-earth God loves us.

Jesus Christ

Jesus Christ is the one whom the Christian church calls Lord. God had tried many ways of bringing his people into loving obedience to him, giving them the Law and sending them the prophets. During the time when Augustus Caesar was ruler of the Roman Empire and Herod was king of Judea, God chose to show his nature and purpose to his people in a new way. He took upon himself human form. . .and entered earthly life in the Babe of Bethlehem, Jesus, child of Mary. This does not mean that God's presence and power was limited to this human form; he was still Lord of all his world. But the fullness of God was also seen in Jesus who grew as other children, living in the carpenter's household at Nazareth.

Jesus was about thirty years old when he left Nazareth. He was seen among the crowds following John, a preacher of repentance who was baptizing people as a sign of the forgiveness of their sins. Jesus, too, was baptized, and this seems to have been a sign of a special calling. A Voice said,

"Thou art my beloved Son; with thee I am well pleased." (Mark 1:11.) Followers gathered around him as he returned to Galilee. He chose twelve men as special disciples. Wherever he went, crowds gathered. The message he gave them was: "Good news! The rule of God is in your midst." The signs of the Kingdom were the crowds, eager for his words, the healing of the sick, and the casting out of demons. . . . Jesus called people to a keeping of the Law, which demanded complete surrender to God. A person could not do this himself [or herself]: only by the indwelling Spirit of God could such a life be possible.

Jesus' criticism of the leaders among his people, as well as his own interpretations of the Law, aroused the anger of the leaders. Moreover, they feared that the enthusiastic crowds might bring suspicion from the Roman rulers. Who was this man Jesus? Some said he was a prophet—even the forerunner of the promised Messiah. Others said that he might be the Messiah: one sent of God to free his people from the conquering rule of Rome. When Jesus asked the Twelve who they thought he was, Peter answered, "You are the [Messiah] Christ. . . ."

The crowds were turning away, and the rulers were plotting Jesus' downfall. Jesus and his disciples went to Jerusalem for the Passover festival. . . . On Thursday evening of that week, he ate a Passover meal with his disciples. . . . That evening he was betrayed by Judas, one of the Twelve, tried before the religious rulers and the Roman governor, and the next day was crucified. But to those who had believed that he was indeed God's Son and the promised One, he appeared, raised from the dead. . . . Finally, he appeared to a large group of followers, telling them that he was returning to his Father and they would see him no more, but that he would send the Holy Spirit in his place. . . .

Christians see Jesus' whole life from the perspective of his risen glory. The story of his life is written in four books which are called Gospels, writings setting forth the "good news." Many titles have been given to him. His given name, "Jesus" (in Hebrew, "Joshua"), means "he who saves." The title that his followers use, "Christ" (in Hebrew, "Messiah"), means "one anointed" by God's call. He is known as Son of Man, Son of God, Redeemer, Savior. In his own day he was called "Rabbi," which means "Teacher," and "Master," which means "Lord." But since "Lord" was also the name used to call upon God, the followers of Jesus (after his resurrection) were affirming by the title that there was a special relationship between God and Jesus Christ. Their name for him was "Lord Jesus," and they were willing to live and to die for him because they knew that he had saved them from sin, that he loved them, and that he had given them eternal life.[1]

8

Does God Know How We Feel?

Do you think God knows what it's like
—to be lonely?
—to feel the warmth of friend-ship?
—to be rejected by one's friends?
—to feel like everyone thinks you're a failure?
—to be a human being with sexual feelings?
—to be hurt?
—to feel sadness and grief?
—to feel joy and excitement?
—to struggle with temptations?
—to be confused?
The Incarnation means that God knows what it's like to be a human being. God knows what the ups and downs and in-betweens of our lives feel like from the inside. The Gospels tell us that in Jesus, God became human. The Gospels also tell us that Jesus had ups and downs and in-betweens. So God knows how sorrows and failures can crush us. God also knows how joys and successes can refresh our spirits and make life great fun. That's worth remember-ing the next time you feel like you're drowning in sadness or bubbling over with happiness or torn apart by temptations. God understands how you feel and wants to share with you the bad as well as the good.

It Makes a Difference

Jesus' message in the Gospels is an announcement and a challenge: "Things are different now. I have come. I speak and act for my heavenly Father. God's kingdom is within your reach. Grab hold of it! Change the direction of your life. Trust me and accept the new life God offers you." That is the message spoken in Palestine two millennia ago and, through the Bible, spoken to us today.

But what does it mean? How would it change our lives if we took the message seriously? We may be able to learn from the example of ordinary people who themselves took Jesus' message seriously—for instance, Kelli Duchak.

It all started when Kelli . . . was in the seventh grade. She joined a Bible study led by two eleventh grade girls. She looked up to them, not just because they were juniors, but because they taught her about the Christian faith and lived the faith they talked about.

Kelli decided that, when she got to high school, she too would lead a Bible study. She wanted to share with others the happiness and love the two juniors, Kelly and Margaret, had given her.

For the past two and a half years, Kelli has met regularly with "her girls." She started the Bible study during her sophomore year with one seventh grade girl.

"Within a short period of time, I had five girls," said the eighteen-year-old from Tipp City, Ohio, near Dayton.

The purpose of her Bible study, Kelli explained, is to teach the girls about Jesus and to give them a place where they can talk about their problems and their joys. Kelli tries to provide them with a role model for living the Christian life as a teenager. But she especially tries to be a loving and caring friend to the younger girls. . . .

Kelli knows from personal experience that middle school can be a tough time in your life. She remembers the hurt she felt in the sixth grade when her parents divorced. She also remembers being low in the self-confidence department while she was in middle school.

"I hated the way I looked and my family life," Kelli recalled. "I thought I was nobody."

Her Christian faith, though, helped her through the hard times and gave her a more positive outlook on life. . . .

Leading the Bible study has not always been fun and easy. Covering topics such as jealousy, boyfriends, gossip, parents, self-confidence, and Bible stories has required planning and preparation.

"My biggest interest has been working and serving with my youth group," said Kelli. "It has been where I've spent my time and energy since the seventh grade when I first joined. The biggest reason I became so involved was the people, who spent time with me, cared about me, and just plain loved me as I was. Because of that,

others, by spending time alone with God, by being positive, and by laughing at lot."[2]

Can you think of other persons—whom you know or know about—who have responded to Jesus' announcement and example? What evidence can you point to? (Have you heard them talk about their faith? Have you noticed a change in their behavior?)

What difference could it make in your life if *you* responded to Jesus' announcement and example?

God gave me a heart that wanted to give all of that back to other people."

Kelli's youth group has provided her with lots of opportunities for doing just that. One was a Habitat for Humanity mission project in New York City.

"We helped build an apartment, we painted, and did every kind of dirty work imaginable," Kelli said. "We worked side by side with people from the slums, with different nationalities and races, and in a culture that is like nothing I've ever imagined. I realized there that the best feeling in the world is knowing you gave up parts of yourself to make other people happy. . . ."

According to Kelli, "People look at the way you live, not at what you preach, and from there decide about their own lives. I practice my faith by loving and serving

[1] From *An Introductory Theological Wordbook*, by Iris V. and Kendig Brubaker Cully (The Westminster Press, 1943); pages 101–103.
[2] Reprint from *The Magazine for Christian Youth!*, May, 1988, pages 41–42. Copyright © 1988 by Graded Press.

Chapter 2

What Makes Jesus So Special? (continued)

CORNERSTONE

Jesus is special because of the Atonement. By his life and especially by his death and resurrection, Jesus Christ has overcome our separation from God and from one another.

Your God Is Too Wimpy

"We have turned Jesus into a warm fuzzy," William J. O'Malley writes in the Jesuit periodical *America*. "In reacting against the overly restrictive and punitive God many of us were introduced to in our childhood, we have come full cycle in the other direction: from Molech [the national god of the Ammonites to whom children were sacrificed] to Milquetoast [synonymous with being soft, a patsy]." O'Malley, who teaches at McQuaid Jesuit High School in Rochester, New York, says that over the past ten years he has read some 80,000 pages of students' reflections on God and the church." O'Malley says, "Only last week, one of my students wrote: 'I had—and still have to some degree—the assumption that you can treat God like a wimp. Like I can do whatever I want, and He'll just forget about it, no matter how I really feel. . . . It really isn't possible to have a relationship with a wimpy God.'"[1]

Discussion Questions

(1) Is it possible to respect a God who doesn't seem to care what we do? Why or why not?

(2) There's a saying: "You get out of something as much as you put into it." What does this say about following a wimpy God?

(3) Give several examples from your own life of how God is not a wimp that indicate God's strength of caring.

Sacrifice

A sacrifice is an offering or gift made to God. The purpose is to have communion with God or to make an offering for sin. In the Old Testament a sacrifice might be made in behalf of an individual or of the whole people. There were daily sacrifices and those made on special festival days. The sacrifice was always made at a holy place, such as the Tabernacle or Temple and was offered by a priest in behalf of the people. It should be noted that a sacrifice was never a way of buying forgiveness, for that is a gift of God. It could only express sorrow for sins committed unknowingly. Most sacrifices were of animals, but the meal and wine offerings symbolized other foods used by [people]. Sometimes the entire offering was burned; sometimes parts became the portion of the priests for their own food. . . .

The sacrificial ceremonies were interrupted by the exile in Babylon, restored when the Temple was rebuilt at Jerusalem about a century later, and finally came to an end with the destruction of that Temple in A.D. 70.

Sometimes the Old Testament writers saw the inadequacies of the sacrificial system. The psalmist knew that a holy life was more acceptable to God than any sacrifice. But the Christians were the first people in the ancient world to abandon the idea of animal sacrifice. They saw in the death of Jesus a pure and perfect sacrifice. He was the lamb substituted for sinful people. He was the ransom through whom his people were freed. His resurrection was the joyful sign of an acceptable sacrifice. One of the meanings of the Lord's Supper is a remembrance of the death of Jesus, an offering of God himself through which [men and women are] brought into a new relationship with God.[2]

Biblical Images of the Atonement

Jesus Christ is given names or titles that are descriptive of his role in the Atonement, that shed light on how he restored the brokenness of humankind. Choose one name from the list below, read the Bible reference, and then jot down some notes on how this dimension of Jesus Christ relates to the Atonement:

☐ Suffering Servant . . . Isaiah 53
☐ The High Priest . . Hebrews 4:14
☐ The Lamb of God . . John 1:29
☐ The Bread of Life . . John 6:35
☐ The Resurrection and the Life . . . . John 11:25
☐ The Mediator . . 1 Timothy 2:5
☐ Our Passover . . 1 Corinthians 5:7
☐ Redeemer . . . . Job 19:25
☐ Savior . . . . 1 John 4:14
☐ The Good Shepherd . . . . John 10:11
☐ The Vine . . . . John 15:5

A Candid Look at the Atonement

Okay, I admit it. I don't really understand this Atonement stuff. I've heard different theories trying to explain how God did it. Is only one right? Or are all of them partly wrong?

How exactly did Jesus save us from our sins? Was it a ransom payment? Some evil being sent God this ransom note (there had to be a note—there always is on television mysteries):

"Dear Mr. G: We're holding everybody on earth hostage and won't let them go until you send us the most precious thing you have. That's right. We want your Son. Specific instructions will fol-

low this note. You will obey them explicitly. Signed, the Prince of Darkness."

"Dear Mr. G: (our apologies if it's something other than Mr.) Leave your only Son in the little village of Bethlehem, and don't call in the authorities. We want this whole operation to be low key. A manger would do nicely, and throw in a few cows and donkeys plus a shepherd or two if you like. We'll be watching for a sign of your compliance. Signed, the Fallen Archangel."

"Dear Mr. G: We said low key; so what was this business of a brightly shining star, King Herod, wise men from distant lands? You better play it straight or the deal is off. And you may as well know that lots of people are expecting this

Son of yours to come through by freeing them from Roman occupation. Well, if he doesn't, I won't be responsible for what happens to him. Signed, the Evil Instigator."

God did send his Son, and the rest (as they say) is history. Jesus didn't do what the folks in power wanted, and God ended up paying the ultimate price. The death of God's beloved Son was what ransomed us from sin and death and released goodness into our lives. This theory recognizes that sin is a serious problem. God is holy, neither a wimp nor a pushover. But this theory has its limitations too. It makes the whole business seem a little mechanical, like a business or a legal deal between divine and demonic powers. Where is the place for our personal decisions of faith?

Let's try the next explanation, the moral influence theory. God, who once destroyed everything by a flood (with a few notable exceptions such as Mr. and Mrs. Noah and an ark full of animals) decided to be Mr. Nice Guy and to convince people to be loving and kind. So he sent his Son, Jesus, to teach and heal and set a good example for all of us. God even allowed him to die on the cross to demonstrate for us the way of sacrificial living. That's a steep price to pay for maybe convincing a few folks to follow along the narrow way. Why not try a little more friendly arm twisting instead

of a crucifixion? And if sin is such a serious problem, wouldn't something more potent than setting a good example be required?

Now we take off on a hunting expedition to substitutionary theory country. Jesus took our place. We deserved to be dispatched for our sins, but Jesus took upon himself the punishment sinful humanity deserved. Check out Isaiah 53 for a solid biblical account. This view assumes that God is angry and wants satisfaction. Jesus somehow pays the price through his suffering and death.

This part I can't figure out. I know how angry I get when some criminal on trial gets off scot-free. It doesn't seem right. So I can understand that God can't let people off with a wink. But even *human* parents can forgive without beating the daylights out of their kids. Shouldn't God be able to do that much? Of course, it helps when you remember that God wasn't just sitting back, watching things happen. God was the one doing the suffering and dying too.

Maybe none of these theories is fully adequate. Suppose we patch them together, throw in some healthy skepticism, a pinch of doubt, and a whole parcel of awe and wonder. Then we better take off our shoes 'cause we're treading on holy ground here; we're approaching the sacred mystery of the Atonement. The only thing we can be absolutely sure of is that somehow Jesus' life and death and resurrection make possible our at-one-ment with God.

Reconciliation First, Other Stuff Later

It wasn't my fault. It wasn't her's either. It really wasn't anybody's. We'd been best friends since the second grade—jumped rope for thousands of hours, played hopscotch until the driveway was covered with chalk lines, spent recess together. Then it was listening to tapes together, fixing each other's hair, and shopping at the center like a couple of mall rats.

Maybe we started to drift apart when boys entered the picture. I guess you can't blame guys for everything that goes wrong, although . . . Maybe it was something I said or something I didn't say. We can't even talk to each other any more. We say "hi" when we pass in the hallway, but there's no eye contact; sort of like talking to the wall.

It isn't like I don't have other friends. But she was special, and I thought I was special to her. Other people tell me to forget it; let her make the first move because she caused the break. She did say a bunch of things that hurt, but so did I. I think we were both confused and having a tough time growing up. Surviving age thirteen isn't easy! I remember all too well.

Last Sunday I was sitting on the church pew minding my own business, writing a note to my boy friend, when I heard the minister read from the Bible. I didn't quite catch it all so I looked it up during the sermon. In case you're wondering, I *was* listening. It was a pretty good sermon. Hey, I can walk and chew gum at the same time and study and watch television together so writing a note and hearing a sermon is no problem.

The passage was Matthew 5:23-25: "So if you are offering your gift at the altar, and there remember that your brother [I added sister] has something against you, leave your gift there before the altar and go; first be reconciled to your brother [or sister], and then come and offer your gift. Make friends quickly."

I wondered if God was trying to give me a message when our minister's third point (or fourth or fifth, I'd sort of lost track) was based on 2 Corinthians 5:19-20a: "In Christ God was reconciling the world to himself, not counting their trespasses against them, and entrusting to us the message of reconciliation. So we are ambassadors for Christ, God making his appeal through us."

I knew what I had to do. I telephoned as soon as I got home and set up a time to meet at lunch the next day so we could talk this all out. I felt like a ton of bricks had been lifted off my back. Who knows? We may even become best friends again. Next time I see our pastor, I'm going to compliment her on that sermon!

The Depth of God's Love

When you love someone a great deal, you want the best for him or her. You are constantly looking for ways to express the depth of your feelings. God was so in love with creation, especially the human beings he had fashioned after his own image, that he enjoyed letting them know that fact in a variety of wonderful ways.

But people failed to appreciate God's gifts. They acted selfishly and cruelly. They refused to obey God's law; they rejected his offer of love. God could have decided to start over again. He could have created another planet where the inhabitants would accept him. Instead, he took the initiative. He sent his Son to show us the way back, to restore the broken relationship. Paul makes an eloquent statement to this effect: "In Christ God was reconciling the world to himself, not counting their trespasses against them, and entrusting to us the ministry of reconciliation" (2 Corinthians 5:19).

Motivated by unconditional love, God acted in Jesus to make amends for our sins, to atone for our mistakes. Because of the depth and length and breadth of God's love, we are at-one with him, with all creation, and with one another.

[1] From *The Christian Ministry*, September 1986; page 18.
[2] From *An Introductory Theological Wordbook*, by Iris V. and Kendig Brubaker Cully (The Westminster Press, 1943); pages 179–80.

Chapter 3

Does God Love Us Because We're Good?

CORNERSTONE

We cannot earn God's favor by doing things. We can have a right relationship with God only by God's grace.

Confusing Questions

Lucy's point has a kernel of truth in it. But there is a more profound truth about what Snoopy hopes for. The theological term for it is *grace*.

Who among us would *really* want to get what we deserve—not what we *want*, but what we *deserve*?

The apostle Paul recognized the good news that God does not give us what we deserve. Instead, God loves us graciously. The abundant life (here and hereafter) is made available to us as a gift.

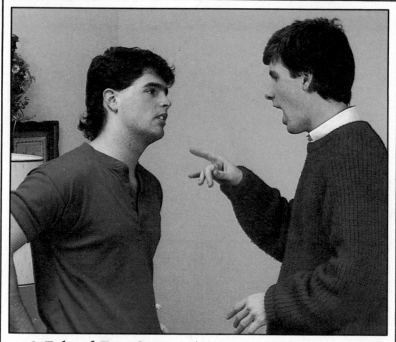

A Tale of Two Sons

You'd have to look a long time before finding two brothers as different from each other as Fred and Terry. The older one, Fred, hardly ever did anything wrong at home or in school. Terry, on the other hand, seemed determined to prove to the world that no one was going to tell him what to do!

Fred thought that Terry was a spoiled, irresponsible brat. And Terry considered Fred to be a boring old stick-in-the-mud.

The episode of the drum set had stuck in Fred's craw for years. It symbolized for him how his parents favored his younger brother. When he was twelve, he'd asked if he could play the drums in the school band. But he'd had to settle for borrowing his cousin's battered saxophone instead. When Terry got to junior high and wanted to play the drums, he was not only allowed to do so but got his own fancy trap set.

As a young adult, Fred lived in their home town and worked hard in the family business. He became a solid, respectable citizen. Terry, bright as he was, wandered from job to job and from town to town. He flunked out of college; his marriage ended in divorce. He decided to move to the other end of the country, as far away from home as he could get. Fred knew that his father had given Terry a substantial amount of money for moving expenses. It brought back memories of the drum set.

Fred kept track of Terry through the occasional letters to his parents. Terry squandered everything and was almost living on the streets when he came to his senses, stopped rebelling, and settled down with a new job and a new family.

"Terry's coming home! He's coming for a visit!" His mother's voice was filled with joy.

"Let's have a family reunion," suggested the father. "We'll invite everybody and have a wonderful party. We haven't seen our Terry in almost ten years."

Fred couldn't handle the festivities. While everyone else was celebrating Terry's return, he stomped out of the house. His parents followed to ask him what the problem might be.

"I'll tell you what's wrong!" The pent-up frustration burst forth. "That other son of yours makes a mess of his life, gives you sleepless nights, wastes your money, and has never been responsible for anything in his whole life. So now he comes home, and what do you do? You throw him a party. He doesn't deserve it."

"But he's our son. We love him and are so happy to have him with us!"

"I'm your son too. I've never done any of the wrong things Terry did. I earned good grades, worked hard, and I never complained about playing that beat up old saxophone either."

What do you think Fred's parents might have said next?

This is a contemporary rendition of one of the parables Jesus told to explain God's love. The original parable of the prodigal son is found in Luke 15:11-32.

The Parable of the Fast Food Laborers

"Come on! We haven't got all day. Speed it up! We need eight more burgers on the double. Get those fries going too. And a little kid just spilled a chocolate shake." The floor supervisor was turning the screws.

It had been a hectic time at Biggie Burger. In addition to the usual traffic, five school buses had pulled in at the busiest time of the dinner rush hour. The staff was worn out from all the running and from the stress as well. The entire week had been tough. They'd exceeded their quota of cantankerous customers, had $50 bills given to pay for $0.60 soft drinks, extra messy tables, huge smudges on the plate glass doors, several total disasters in the rest rooms, and pressure, pressure, pressure. The one redeeming factor was that payday came tomorrow.

As with most fast food franchises, there was a fairly rapid turnover of employees. On Wednesday, one new person had been hired. Then another was added to the crew on Friday. Finally, two more were recruited Saturday night. These two newest employees mostly stood around smiling nervously and wiping already clean counters.

The next day as the pay envelopes were being handed out, the two persons most recently hired exclaimed, "Look how much we got paid! It's a whole week's wages. Wow!"

Well, those who had labored and sweated the entire week figured they'd receive a big bonus. After all, they had worked hard. But when they looked, their pay was exactly the same as the others.

"Hey, what gives? How come they got as much as we got? They only worked four easy hours while we slaved for almost forty.

"Just a minute now. Calm down and think about it," replied the owner. "It's my store, isn't it? Can't I do with my money what I wish? And anyway, didn't I pay you what your contract calls for?"

"Yes, but you paid them . . ."

"No but's about it. I can be generous and gracious to whomever I choose."

Then the owner added this wonderfully strange saying: "So the last shall be first, and the first last."

The workers puzzled over the meaning of that phrase for the remainder of their work shift.

This is a contemporary rendition of one of the parables Jesus told to explain God's love. The original parable of the laborers in the vineyard is found in Matthew 20:1-16.

The Meaning of Grace

"Grace" is . . . the most important word in the Protestant vocabulary. It is also the most abused. We have difficulty in answering why the rallying cry of the Reformers should have been *salvatio sola gratia* (salvation by grace alone). And yet the destiny of Protestantism is bound up with that affirmation. Grace cannot really be described, it can only be experienced. All we can do is try to describe what is experienced.

1. We miss the point if we talk in abstract terms. For grace, in Christian terms, is not the least bit abstract: it is very specific. It is *the grace of our Lord Jesus Christ*. We cannot talk about grace apart from him. The prologue to the Fourth Gospel reminds us that "the law was given through Moses, but grace and truth came through Jesus Christ" (John 1:17). Paul stresses this even more than the author of the Fourth Gospel, and it is not surprising that the Reformers leaned heavily upon him. For Paul, the heart of the gospel is "the grace of God which was given you in Christ Jesus (1 Cor. 1:4). When he blesses the Corinthian church, he makes grace pivotal for everything else: "The grace of our Lord Jesus Christ, and the love of God, and the communion of the Holy Spirit, be with you all" (2 Cor. 13:14). Grace is defined by who Jesus Christ is, or better, by what Jesus Christ does. He is the one who transforms grace from an idea into a reality. To understand grace we must look . . . to a life lived, a death died, a grave overcome. Grace and truth came through Jesus Christ. . . .

2. "The grace of our Lord Jesus Christ" is not a "thing," an object, an impersonal something or other. It can only be described in personal terms. Grace is not something God himself gives us, it is the way God gives us himself. Grace is *God's personal relationship to us*. But his relationship to us is unlike most of the human relationships we experience, and we must distinguish carefully between them.

Some human relationships are based on *merit*: a baseball club employs a player because he can hit .340 or is exceptionally adept with a glove. Some relationships are based on *need*: I get acquainted with a garage mechanic because he can fix my broken carburetor, or I get acquainted with a banker because he can help me stay solvent. Some relationships are based on *appeal*: a man does not love a woman because she can fix his carburetor or help him stay solvent, but because he finds her beautiful, or appealing, or exciting to be with. (He may even be so swept off his feet by her that he ends his sentences with prepositions.)

The relationship based on grace is unlike the relationship based on merit or need or appeal. God does not enter into personal relationship with his children because they are "good." They are not. Nor does he do so because he "needs" them. He does not. He is not gracious to them because they are "appealing." They are not. Quite the contrary. The Bible is emphatic in asserting that God's relationship to [humanity] is not based on the fact that [we] offer something to God, but on the fact that God offers everything to [us]. God does not love Israel because Israel is a great or good nation. Israel, as a matter of fact, is an insignificant nation and (by all normally accepted standards of judgment) a bad nation. And yet God loves Israel . . . simply because he loves Israel. That is the kind of God he is. . . .

3. We can discover two further things about "the grace of our Lord Jesus Christ" but they must always be mentioned together.

First of all, we learn that grace is *mercy* or *forgiveness*. "While we were yet sinners" was the time God visited us with his grace, and, instead of condemning us, forgave us. We get an inkling of what this means even on the human level. If I have willfully hurt someone, and thus destroyed our relationship, what I "deserve" is to be condemned and punished. This will never heal the hurt or restore the relationship, and the hurt can be healed, the relationship restored, only when the one who has been wronged is willing to bear the pain of having been wronged, and yet forgive me. Nothing I can do will ever be enough, no matter how hard I try. Mercy and forgiveness must come from the one I have hurt. The most I can do is to accept forgiveness when it is offered, realizing that I do not really deserve it.

That is how Protestantism explains the relationship between God and [human beings]. We have wilfully "hurt" God, and thus destroyed our relationship with him. We have spurned him, sinned against his children, answered his love by our hate. And what can overcome love answered by hate? Grace, and grace alone: grace as mercy, grace as forgiveness, grace that bears the hurt in suffering love, grace, in short, made real upon a cross.

Because it is mercy and forgiveness, grace is also *power*. It is the gift of new life. The one who has been forgiven lives in a new situation. Paul reports the word from on high that came to him: "My grace is sufficient for you; for my power is made perfect in weakness" (2 Cor. 12:9). The weakness of the human frame becomes the channel of divine power, so that new energies are unleashed. The recipient of the power will need, of course, to remember its source, and Paul himself could come close to forgetting this. "I worked harder than any of them," he boasted before he caught himself and described what this actually meant, "though it was not I, but the grace of God which is with me" (1 Cor. 15:10).[1]

---

[1] From *The Spirit of Protestantism*, by Robert McAfee Brown (Oxford University Press, 1961); pages 53–57.

Chapter 4

Does God Love Us Because We're Good?
(continued)

CORNERSTONE

Good works spring from gratitude for God's grace. God cares a great deal about how we live each day. As Christians, however, we respond to God's expectations, not from fear, but with love.

Grace Is Not Cheap

Life holds important lessons for both Fred and Terry. Being the older brother who acts so responsibly, Fred believes that people should get what they deserve. If you study and work hard and stay out of trouble, then your life should go fairly smoothly. But if you goof around and do as little as possible, Fred figures that your reward will be hardship and heartache.

However, life is not that simple! Sometimes good people have bad times, and the foolish ones sail through the years. In Chapter 3, we read how hard it was for Fred to accept that his parents could be so forgiving and loving to his younger brother, Terry. Terry had made a mess of things but finally came home to become part of the family again. Fred saw his parents' acceptance of Terry as unjust.

Like these forgiving parents, God is full of grace. Grace means God's love offered to make our lives whole. Grace is *prevenient*; that is, God offers grace before we do anything to deserve it. Grace is what makes Christians tick. Grace is the foundation of our lives. A converted slave trader wrote two hundred years ago,

Amazing grace! how sweet the sound
That saved a wretch like me!
I once was lost, but now am found,
Was blind, but now I see.[1]

But what about Terry? Does the story of grace end with the comforting announcement that God accepts us all, no matter what? Does Terry then go on his merry way living irresponsibly? What else might Christian faith involve beyond being freed from religious legalism?

Living by God's loving grace does indeed free us, but it is a freedom *to* as well as a freedom *from*. Being free from earning salvation, we are thus free to follow Christ, gratefully, by serving.

New life in Christ is full of love but still demands something from us. Christians cannot avoid this tension; it will always be part of our lives. Yet, it is a dynamic tension that will help us grow in faith and help us give more and more of ourselves to the One who gave himself for us.

Terry returned to the fold. He received the overwhelming joy that his parents and friends offered. Now what? How will Terry continue his life? Will there be any changes?

This question must remain open. God does not force us to serve, any more than God forces us to take the grace of Jesus Christ. We have a clue to an answer, though, because Fred and Terry's story was first told in the Gospel of Luke. We know it as the parable of the prodigal son (Luke 15:11-32). The key comes in the middle of that story, as Jesus says, "But when he came to himself . . ." (verse 17).

When he came to himself! The difference between death and life rests on this phrase. It reminds us that grace is not a one-way street. We must respond in order to receive. The prodigal son came to his senses and realized what a mess he had made. His only way out was to change. The road home symbolizes his acceptance of the expectations of grace. God's love does not let us go, does not let us down, and does not let us off!

God expects something from you too. God is calling you to follow and serve Jesus Christ. Before this can happen, you must admit that you do not live up to God's expectations. Whether you think that you are good, bad, or in-between, you need to face your failure at obeying the law. Then you are ready to decide what you are going to do about it: continue as you are or follow Christ. If you have never told God that you are Christ's disciple, make that your next step (don't worry about how you say it—just pray it silently).

Following Christ is a journey through your entire lifetime. It's a path in which you think, feel, decide, and act based on being thankful, not fearful. Every day you can tell God that you want to live that day because you are glad, glad for grace.

Remind yourself about something else too from time to time. Life in grace always means some tension—between *wanting* to and *having* to. That tension will never go away completely. With God's grace, however, even that tension has creative possibilities.

Set Free to Serve

Nancy closed the door of the "Golden Years Retirement Club" behind her. It marked the end of a chapter in her life that she would like to forget.

The trouble began two months ago, when she and several of her friends had strolled to the end of a pier that jutted out from the park into the river. They were alone. Phyllis had a joint, and they were sharing it when a young man in jeans and a T-shirt that said "Have a Nice Day" began walking towards them. A moment of panic clutched Nancy, but she soon relaxed, since he looked harmless. By the time he reached them, it was too late. "You're under arrest," he said firmly.

Then came the ride to the police station, the phone call to her parents, and the scene that followed when they all reached home. Nancy's parents had not suspected she smoked pot, and she had never even come close to being arrested before.

The day she went to court Nancy experienced a mixture of fear and surprise. Nancy and her friends had expected a fine, but instead they were sentenced to work for ten hours at a home for senior citizens. Nancy would have preferred a fine!

Every Sunday afternoon for five weeks she was to appear at Pinecrest Home for Adults. She was assigned to the club that provided recreation for the more active residents.

The first afternoon passed slowly. Nancy knew no one, and

she had talked to very few old people before. She was nervous and quiet, and left with a feeling of relief. Only four more visits.

But then something happened. On her second visit, Nancy discovered she remembered several people's names, and she enjoyed calling out the numbers for Bingo. One very friendly woman named Mrs. Brenner admired the sweater Nancy was wearing, and they discussed a knitting project they could work on together. The hours passed so quickly that Nancy was surprised when it was time to go home.

Now it was all over. She could try to forget the embarrassment of what had brought her to the Pinecrest Home in the first place. No more Sunday afternoons with all those old people. Her time was her own. She was free again!

As she had prepared to leave, Mr. Forlano, the director, had seemed sad. "You know, Nancy," he told her, "you're one of the best volunteers we've ever had. Everyone has taken to you. We're going to miss you. I wish we weren't saying goodbye." Nancy remembered the tears in Mrs. Brenner's eyes when she explained that it was her last afternoon.

"But I'm free!" she said to herself. "I'm free." She paused for a few moments, then turned and opened the door. The director was at his desk just inside. "Mr. Forlano," she said, "I want to be a regular volunteer."

Nancy learned something very important from her work at the Retirement Club. She learned that there are actually two kinds of freedom.

The first is freedom *from*—freedom understood as liberation from circumstances which seem to be oppressive or stifling. When the people of Israel escaped from their slavery in Egypt, they were experiencing this sort of freedom. For the first time in their lives, they knew what it was like to be rid of their burdens. Nancy discovered the same kind of freedom when she realized that she no longer had to work with the elderly people to whom she had been assigned. As long as her work was the result of a judge's sentence, she was not free to do what she wanted with her Sunday afternoons. It was only when she walked out of the club at the end of her ten hours of work that she was free from the restrictions that had dictated her sentence.

But the remarkable thing that occurred to Nancy as she left the Retirement Club was that she didn't have to leave at all. She was free from her duties, but she had also received another kind of freedom. She had freedom *for*—freedom for choosing what she would and would not do. Her decision to return to work as a volunteer represented this different kind of freedom—the freedom to choose.

Christians consider this second kind of freedom to be the most precious of God's gifts to the human family, because we share that freedom with God.[2]

Side-by-Side Comparison of Law and Grace

Law	Grace
conformity	creativity
written codes	the law written in the heart
competition with others	a desire to cooperate with others
peer pressure	a feeling of peer support
a sense of duty	inner discipline
doing the minimum	wanting to do the maximum
have to, ought, and must	want to, may I, joyful response
fulfilling requirements	being spontaneous and creative

Paraphrase of Romans 6:1-2, 15

So tell me what you think. Is it okay for us to keep on sinning so God will be able to show us more kindness and forgiveness? No way! That's like playing games with God about something very important: our relationship to him. God can't be manipulated like that.

Yes, no matter how many times we sin and no matter how rotten we behave, God will forgive us. But that doesn't mean sin is to be taken lightly. Our sin hurts us and others too and disappoints God.

Just because our salvation depends on God's grace doesn't mean we can do what we jolly well please. In Christ we have been set free to love and to do good.

Paraphrase of James 2:14-26

What good does it do, my friends, if a person says "I have faith" but never does any good deeds to demonstrate it? Can just talking about how wonderful our relationship to God is save us? If poor, hungry persons come and one of you says, "Go in peace; everything's cool; pretend you've got lots of food and a warm place to sleep" but fails to give them any concrete assistance for their physical needs, big deal! Faith by itself, if it doesn't offer concrete help, is deader than a doorknob.

Somebody is sure to say that faith and good works have nothing to do with each other. Baloney, I say. The two go together like a horse and carriage, like love and marriage.

Some famous people of faith demonstrated the connection a long time ago. Abraham did when he was willing to give up his only son, Isaac. And Rahab, whose reputation wasn't very good, showed her faith when she risked hiding Israelite spies. Just like a body is a lifeless bunch of chemical elements without the spirit, so faith without good works is dead.

Christmas Day in the Morning

Rob absolutely hated to get up in the morning. But on the farm he was expected to rise by 5:00 A.M. to help his father with the chores. Rob usually fell out of bed with his eyes half-closed and stumbled to the barn, grumbling every step of the way. Then one year on the day before Christmas, Rob overheard his dad tell his mother how he wished he could let Rob sleep in just once.

In a flash of insight Rob realized how much his father loved him. As the author Pearl Buck so beautifully tells the story, Rob wished with all his heart that he could buy his dad a really good present.[3] Rob had scraped some loose change together and had bought a cheap tie. However, now that he felt this deep bond of love, Rob wanted to get something much better. But there was neither time nor money.

Rob had an idea. When he went to bed that Christmas Eve, he had it all figured out. It would be a special gift! He lay awake and gazed out the window at the stars twinkling overhead. One star was so brilliant he wondered if it might actually be the star of Bethlehem. Every so often he dozed off, then awakened with a start and lit a match to check his watch. It was 1:00 A.M., then 1:30, 2:00, 2:20, 2:45. By 3:00 A.M., he could stand it no longer. He quietly slipped down the stairs, careful to miss the squeaky spots, and made his way to the barn. The cows were surprised to see him so early. He made all the preparations, milked the cows (it was the first time he'd ever done it all by himself), put the cans away, and cleaned up.

Rob returned to his room and barely had time to jump under the covers when he heard his father coming.

"Son, it's time to get up to do the chores. I know it's Christmas, but the cows need to be milked anyway."

Rob waited expectantly, his heart pounding. Soon he heard his father's footsteps coming again down the hall. Rob pretended to be asleep. His father pulled off the covers, gave Rob a big hug, and said, "Son, no one ever gave me a nicer gift. I love you!" It was dark, but Rob thought he saw tears trickling down his dad's face.

Rob nearly burst with pride as his dad told the rest of the family about how sleepy old Rob had gotten up by himself. The farmhouse was full of Christmas joy as everyone crowded around the festive tree to open presents.

Rob would long remember this particular Christmas, for it was when he gave his first gift of love.

---

[1] From "Amazing Grace! How Sweet the Sound," *The Book of Hymns*, No. 92.

[2] Reprinted from *A Faith for Teenagers* by John Kater, available from Cowley Publications, 980 Memorial Drive, Cambridge, MA 02138 (copyright 1987); pages 149–152.

[3] For Pearl Buck's full version of this story, see "Christmas Day in the Morning," in *The World's Christmas*, edited by Olive Wyon (Fortress Press, 1964). Your church or public library will probably have a copy.

Chapter 5

How Do We Know What Is Right and Wrong?

CORNERSTONE

Christians discover in Scripture general principles for guiding our decisions and actions.

Confusing Questions

According to the Bible, living rightly means obeying God. But how can we know what it means to obey God?

We rightly believe that when people are doing what God intends, life in creation expresses the goodness of God. Instead of making our existence dull, moral behavior is needed to usher God's best options for us into life. Living morally is not a style of living that squeezes all the joy out of us. Rather, it is a way of living that helps open up the highest potentials for human beings.

One of Christian faith's central affirmations, then, is that God wants to create well-being for all. As a banner for motivating Christians, this idea is positive and enthusiastic. And yet, we return to the point from which we began: How do we know *what* it is that God wants us to do? What kind of behavior is right or good? What kind is wrong or bad?

Benchmarks: The Ten Commandments

As Christians, we are not left floating on the stormy sea without steering equipment. The Scriptures provide us with a number of general rules and principles that have not lost their value even today. Let's look first at the Ten Commandments.

The Ten Commandments are the Bible's earliest set of religious and ethical requirements (see Exodus 20:1-17 or Deuteronomy 5:7-11). These *laws*, as they came to be known, were the basic standard of religion and behavior for the people of Israel. Jesus said and did nothing to diminish the value of these ten statements. Jews and Christians still follow them.

A POSITIVE STATEMENT OF THE TEN COMMANDMENTS

The first four commandments deal with our relationship to God.

1 Worship and serve God alone.

2 Human beings are the only proper images of God. Be God's faithful representatives on earth.

3 Use God's name for worthy purposes only.

4 Rejoice in the Lord and rest from labor regularly.

The last six commandments deal with our relationships with other people.

5 Honor your parents and see to their needs.

6 Show respect and reverence for life.

7 Honor and uphold marital love.

8 Respect the goods of others.

9 Speak the truth before the courts and in public life.

10 Be content with what you have. Take pleasure in others' enjoyment of goods and possessions.

Cry for Justice

The great prophets of Israel, such as Amos, Isaiah, Jeremiah, and Hosea, were eloquent spokespersons for moral behavior. They cried out for justice: that homeless persons be helped, lonely persons be loved, the hungry fed. Often in dramatic fashion—for example, ripping their clothing and pouring ashes over their heads—the prophets spoke for God, calling the community of faith to moral living.

Amos used strong language to denounce the greed of the wealthy and their oppression of the poor. He had a marvelous vision of a time when justice will "roll down like waters, and righteousness like an everflowing stream" (Amos 5:24).

Isaiah pleaded with the people to stop rebelling against God's will. He urged them to be good stewards of creation, to become humble servants, and to cease from violent ways.

Jeremiah began his ministry as a very young man (Jeremiah 1:4-10). His message to the nation was to trust in God and not in foreign alliances and in military defenses.

Hosea proclaimed a poignant story of God's unconditional love for us even when we are unfaithful to God and to one another.

The ancient prophets took seriously the problem of individual and corporate immorality and condemned both with all their energy and creativity.

Blueprint of
Scriptural Morality

THE PROPHETS
[Amos 8:10-12; Isaiah 10:1-3;
Micah 4:3, Jeremiah 6:11-14]

LOVE OF OUR NEIGHBORS
[Romans 13:8-10]

**PARABLE OF THE GOOD
SAMARITAN**
[Luke 10:25-37]

TWO GREAT COMMANDMENTS
[Matthew 22:35-40]

JESUS' SERMON ON THE MOUNT
[Matthew 5–7]

DOING GOOD WORKS
[James 2:14-17]

TEN COMMANDMENTS
[Exodus 20:1-17]

The Kids Who
Saved a Town

The *Reader's Digest* reported about a group of young people who literally saved the community of Royston, Georgia, from a slow and lingering death. The downtown was decaying, with a pile of rusting junk cars on a lot, litter scattered all over, buildings with paint peeling off, and numerous vacant stores.

Alice Terry's class of gifted students at Royston School decided somebody needed to do something. They organized and began making phone calls to business people and politicians. The young people begged, nagged, got angry—but they got results. Calling themselves RIPPLES (for the ripple effect they hoped to start), they became the motivating force behind the revitalization of an entire town.

They proved a force to be reckoned with: threatening legal action when all else failed, taking a survey of the people's need for retail establishments, drawing up a proposal for one of the old buildings, and finally pitching in to help pull weeds, pick up garbage, and sweep sidewalks.

The whole community started to work together. A new sense of pride began to grow. As a result of the young people's survey, a discount drugstore decided to come to Royston; so did a large supermarket.

Five students and their teacher, convinced of what was the right thing to do, made all the difference in a town of nearly 3,000 people. The class was honored in Washington, D.C., and received a commendation from the Secretary of the Interior.

Sam's Story

Mrs. Roberts was overjoyed. By adding a gift of money for her birthday to what she'd saved from her social security check, she had just enough to buy a new dress. She knew exactly what she wanted—a wool blend in warm brown tones. The total should come to approximately fifty dollars with tax.

The store at the shopping mall had what she wanted and in her size. What luck! She tried it on to be certain it fit. Did she ever look great in the dressing room mirror!

The clerk totaled the amount. It came to fifty-three dollars, slightly more than Mrs. Roberts had anticipated. The purchase took all her money, including the loose change she found in the bottom of her purse. But she didn't really mind since she'd gotten her beautiful new dress.

Mrs. Roberts hadn't noticed the sale tag on the sleeve. Her eyesight wasn't quite as good as it once had been. And in her excitement she hadn't paid close attention to details. But Samantha, standing in the line behind her, had noticed. The clerk removed the twenty-percent-sale tag quickly and charged the woman full price.

Samantha assumed she wouldn't have to do anything, however, because her minister, Reverend Robinson, was ahead of her in the line. He'd take care of the problem. But he didn't say a word about it as he paid for his white shirt and got the correct discount.

Well, thought Samantha, *the store security guard also noticed. It's his job to correct the error.* But he walked away, acting as though nothing wrong happened. *It's up to me,* Samantha whispered to herself.

Should she say something? Or should she keep quiet? After all, she was only a teenager; and the clerk was more than twice her age. Samantha was scared as she quietly but firmly said, "I think you make a mistake and overcharged that older lady who bought a brown dress. If you'll figure out how much you owe her—it should be about ten dollars—I'll see if I can find her and ask her to come back."

The salesperson didn't appear particularly amused. However, Samantha felt good all over as she escorted Mrs. Roberts back into the store.

"Thank you, young woman. I'd be honored if you'd join me for some ice cream."

"Only if you'll let me pay for my own."

Samantha and Mrs. Roberts walked down the mall toward the sign advertising thirty-three delicious flavors.

This is a contemporary rendition of one of the parables Jesus told. The original parable of the good Samaritan is found in Luke 10:25-37.

Fulfilling the Law of Love

Paul the apostle states in general terms what the good Samaritan parable suggests with its word picture. In Romans, Paul first gives practical advice on how Christians are to behave: Be hospitable, live in peace with all, pray, let God deal with wrong toward yourself, and so on (Romans 12:9-21). He follows this information with a profound summary of what he sees as Christian ethics and its foundation: "Owe no one anything, except to love one another; for he who loves his neighbor has fulfilled the law. The commandments . . . are summed up in this sentence, 'You shall love your neighbor as yourself.' Love does no wrong to a neighbor; therefore love is the fulfilling of the law" (Romans 13:8-10).

Neighborly behavior, then, derives from the intention to fulfill what God expects from those who follow Christ. Love is not a category with specific directions for every possible situation. Love is more a way of life that upholds the ancient commandments and, in the spirit of Christian freedom, is able to deal with circumstances as they arise.

How Firm a Foundation

We can clearly see that the Bible provides a general basis for knowing what is right and wrong. The ancient prohibitions have sound practical and theological purposes for the welfare of humankind. Prophets highlight how those prohibitions translate to doing what is right for all, not for the greed of a few. Jesus draws our attention to the relation between God-love and neighbor-love in some socially surprising ways. Paul struggles to lay out a healthy tension between God-love and following specific demands.

Christians can know what is right and wrong by beginning with this wise witness from the Scriptures.

Chapter 6

How Do We Know What Is Right and Wrong? (continued)

CORNERSTONE

Christian decisions and behavior flow in part from being persons of Christian character.

Not Far Enough

The basis of the moral life, in biblical terms, is obedience to the will of God. We have seen that one way we can know God's will is to examine and apply the rules and principles in Scripture. But that approach does not go quite far enough. For one thing, biblical rules do not cover all the decisions we have to make. These rules were not intended to tell us every detail. They are instead great abiding principles that are for all persons in all situations for all time.

For another thing, God is concerned not only with what we *do* but also with the sort of people we *are*. Christian morality, then, involves our *being* as much as our *doing*. For a more complete answer to the question "What is God's will for us?" we can look to see what the Bible says about *character*. What kind of people does God want us to be?

Transformation

One day a grey-haired caterpillar hanging upside down on a branch surprised her. He seemed caught in some hairy stuff. "You seem in trouble," she said. "Can I help?" "No, my dear, I have to do this to become a butterfly."

Her whole insides leapt. "Butterfly—that word," she thought. "Tell me, sir, what is a butterfly?" "It's what you are meant to become. It flies with beautiful wings and joins the earth to heaven. It drinks only nectar from the flowers and carries the seeds of love from one flower to another."

"Without butterflies the world would soon have few flowers."

"It can't be true!" gasped Yellow. "How can I believe there's a butterfly inside you or me when all I see is a fuzzy worm?"

"How does one become a butterfly?" she asked pensively. "You must want to fly so much that you are willing to give up being a caterpillar."

"You mean to *die*?" asked Yellow, remembering the three who fell out of the sky. "Yes and No," he answered. "What *looks* like you will die but what's *really* you will still live. Life is changed, not taken away. Isn't that different from those who die without ever becoming butterflies?"

"And if I decide to become a butterfly," said Yellow hesitantly. "What do I do?" "Watch me. I'm making a cocoon. It looks like I'm hiding, I know, but a cocoon is no escape. It's an in-between house where the change takes place. It's a big step since you can never return to caterpillar life. During the change, it will seem to you or to anyone who might peek that nothing is happening—but the butterfly is already becoming. It just takes time!"

"And there's something else! Once you are a butterfly, you can *really* love—the kind of love that makes new life. It's better than all the hugging caterpillars can do." "Oh, let me go and get Stripe," Yellow said. But she sadly knew he was too far into the pile to possibly reach. "Don't be sad," said her new friend. "If you change, you can fly and show him how beautiful butterflies are. Maybe he will want to become one too!"

Yellow was torn in anguish: "What if Stripe comes back and I'm not there? What if he doesn't recognize my new self? Suppose he decides to stay a caterpillar? At least we can do *something* as caterpillars—we can crawl and eat. We can love in *some* way. How can two cocoons get together at all? How awful to get stuck in a cocoon!" How could she risk the only life she knew when it seemed so unlikely she could ever be a glorious winged creature? What did she have to go on? —seeing another caterpillar who believed enough to make his own cocoon. —and that peculiar hope which had kept her off the pillar and leapt within her when she heard about butterflies.

The grey-haired caterpillar continued to cover himself with silky threads. As he wove the last bit around his head he called: "You'll be a beautiful butterfly—we're all waiting for you!"[1]

The apostle Paul sees Christian faith as a radical reorientation to life: "Do not be conformed to this world but be transformed by the renewal of your mind, that you may prove what is the will of God, what is good and acceptable and perfect" (Romans 12:2). Christians become a "new creation" in which old things are no longer in effect (2 Corinthians 5:17). The ways that we decide and act are therefore different from the ways of the world in general.

The Apple Tree
(See Matthew 7:17-20)

Quality apples are produced by quality apple trees. A good root system is required so that nutrients can reach the branches and so that the tree can have a solid foundation. A trunk is needed that is not brittle but strong and flexible. The tree must be pruned in such a way as to open all of it to sunlight. Old wood is trimmed to permit new growth where the apple spurs form. Thinning is done in early summer to allow individual apples to achieve the desired size and shape. A tree that is neglected tends to grow many small apples one year and hardly any the next. Many trees require cross-pollination—the pollen from the blossom of a tree of a different variety must be transmitted to their blooms. The tree must also be made resistant to attacks from disease and insects.

A healthy tree produces quality fruit. A tree benefits from having to struggle just a bit. If it has too easy a time—warm weather year round, an abundance of nutrition and water—it may grow lazy and spend too much time looking good. What is desirable is not just lush foliage and supple branches but a good crop of delicious apples.

In like manner, Christian people are known by the quality of the fruit they bear. Do they love others? Are they committed to the cause of justice? Do they show compassion? Are they good stewards of the earth's resources? If a follower of Christ receives adequate spiritual nourishment, is shaped by the master pruner, suffers with Christ over the pain in the world, and is growing and open to new ideas, then a positive, moral life will result. And others will find refreshment and blessing from that person.

By Their Fruits

Jesus did not say, "You can't tell a book by its cover"; but he could have. He taught that the aim for persons is to have their thoughts, feelings, and actions in harmony. The key word is *integrity*. Good actions spring from good motives that come from the personalities of good people. As virtue grows, we do not have to agonize over every decision. Living morally becomes a habit—a positive habit. In addition, as virtue expands within us, our powers of discernment tend to improve.

Music to My Ears

Fifty bucks for a CD player! It's the exact brand and model I've dreamed of having. I could hardly believe my ears when I heard the price. I'd decided that the cost—almost three hundred in the catalogue—was out of my range. A long way out, like in another country or a distant planet. Fifty dollars, however, I could swing. I wonder how those guys can sell it so cheaply? Maybe they got a super good deal. Or maybe I don't want to know.

I had to ask. Sure enough, it's mighty suspicious. It's almost certainly stolen property. There've been a lot of houses broken into lately in our community. The word is that this is part of the haul. I could buy it and nobody would be the wiser. Except I'd have to lie to my friends and my parents. They'd ask, "Where'd you get the great CD player?" I'd make up some phony story; my palms would get sweaty; and I'd have trouble looking them in the eye.

But I want it! Bad! Even more, though, I want to be able to live with myself, to feel good about who I am. And my relationship with Jesus Christ is important too. I don't have any question about what God's Word has to say about this.

I'm going to keep doing odd jobs, earning as much as I can and saving my pennies. When I finally have enough, that CD player will be beautiful music to me in more ways than one.

Discussion Questions

(1) What are sources of pressure that a person of Christian character must sometimes withstand? (peer pressure, the pressure to succeed, wanting material things, undisciplined human or sexual desires)

(2) Should the person in the story have asked what the source of the audio equipment was? Why or why not? Is there ever a situation where ignorance actually is bliss?

(3) Is it just one person against the world when it comes to building Christian character? Or are there persons and groups who can be supportive? List several. (church youth group, church school class, trusted friends, parents, community leaders, respected teachers, and so forth) Are there persons who look to you for guidance and courage?

Set Free Within

I'm absolutely certain I could have pulled it off. Nobody would have seen. I sit one seat behind Elise and one row to her right. It's the perfect position for copying somebody else's work. Elise is a much better student than I am. She's a 4.0, member of the honor society, and English is her strongest subject. Let me tell you—as if you didn't already know—grades are crucial. You've got to have high marks to be admitted to the college you want and to be even considered for scholarships. Plus my parents have expectations! We're talking big time pressure.

I'll be honest. I seriously considered cheating. I mean, I was totally stumped on that one section of the test. Blank brain. A real vacuum head. My final grade was hanging in the balance. An "A" and my grade for the semester would be at least a "B+."

Nobody would ever know. I could put her answers in my own words. So why not do it? After agonizing for what seemed like an eternity, I decided I had to live with myself. I'd know what I did even if no one else did. I'd be cheating myself too. No matter how high my final grade was, I'd know down inside that I hadn't really earned it. And when my parents congratulated me, I'd have wanted to check the floor for dust rather than jump up and down and shout "Hallelujah!"

I know, I know. Everybody else cheats. People lie on their income tax returns, students copy term papers, stuff like that. So why not join the crowd? Because my integrity counts for something. I call myself a Christian; I try to follow Jesus who taught us to be true to ourselves and loving to others. He once said, "You will know the truth, and the truth will make you free" (John 8:32). I value having peace of mind, being free within. Cheating is like stealing thoughts from somebody's mind. And if it became a habit, I'd be robbing from my own future. I wouldn't learn and grow and reach my potential. I'll take an honest "C" any day.

Second Nature

Our decisions and behavior both display and shape our character. Life in faith is a journey; we become more mature and able to act in loving ways. Living a Christian life involves cultivating worthy habits that reflect our faith. And as our character grows, so does our ability to understand intuitively how to see the right and to do it. With this understanding of Christian character, we can appreciate what the great theologian Augustine said years ago about Christian behavior: "Love God and do as you please."

[1] Reprinted from *Hope for the Flowers* by Trina Paulus. © 1972 by Trina Paulus. Used by permission of Paulist Press.

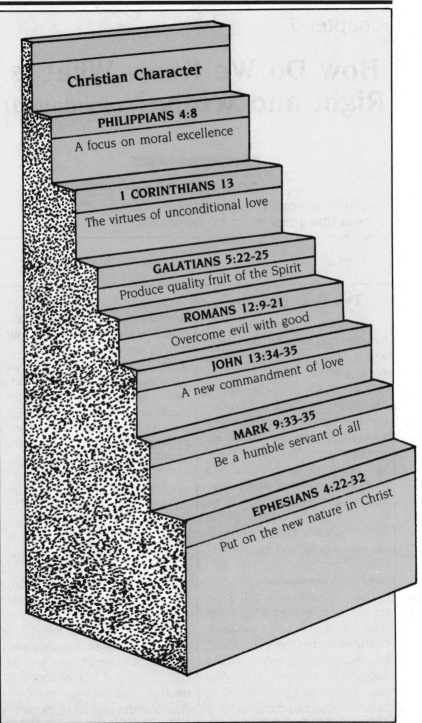

Chapter 7

How Do We Know What Is Right and Wrong? (continued)

CORNERSTONE

Christian morality is rooted in gratitude for the forgiveness that frees us to be responsible.

Two Peas in a Pod

Freedom and responsibility are two sides of one coin; two peas in a pod. They go together like a horse and carriage, hitched so that where one goes, the other is always there. Living a Christian life does indeed mean freedom—we are free to be our true selves, free to entertain new ideas, free to risk loving all people. But this freedom does not mean license. Following Jesus liberates us to act according to the leading of our own conscience. Yet, precisely because we love and care about others, we voluntarily and willingly limit our freedom.

The questions are "When do we do so?" and "How much?" When does our neighbor-love outweigh the rights we have as individuals? How much of our freedom should we yield for the sake of others? Paul offers clues on the way to balance these two dimensions of our lives. In Romans 14:13-23, he suggests that if another person might be injured by one of our actions, we ought to refrain from doing it even though it would not harm us. Paul is specifically referring to eating habits, but the implications are for any behavior that might cause another person to stumble on his or her faith journey.

" 'All things are lawful for me,' " writes Paul, "but not all things are helpful" (1 Corinthians 6:12a). As Christians, we value persons (including ourselves) more highly than food or any other material thing. We seek at all times to do what is best for people, even for the whole world. What we think, say, and do is to build up the quality of human life in the global community. When freedom and responsibility are like two friendly peas in one pod and are kept in a creative tension, both the individual and the group are blessed.

Blue Jeans

The senior high youth choir at Pennington Circle Church has agreed to lead a service of worship at a local retirement home. At the end of the final rehearsal before the service, the issue of what to wear comes up.

Henry: We're all going to wear jeans, right?

Jamal: Well, I figured we'd wear the same kind of clothes we wear to church since it's a worship service.

Pat: How about our nicest jeans?

Marie: Are we doing this for the people at the home, or for ourselves? You know lots of those people will be distracted if we don't dress up. They won't even pay attention to our singing.

Henry: I'm not sure about that. I have an aunt who's in a home and she's pretty up to date. She never complains about me wearing jeans.

Jamal: But she's probably the exception. Most people from that generation still think you should dress up for church. I think we should wear our church clothes....

Marie: It's not going to kill us to dress up for an hour.

Pat: It's not going to kill us, but I think we should be able to wear what we want. It doesn't say anywhere in the Bible that you should dress up for church. We can worship God no matter what we wear.

Henry: That's right. It's what we do that counts. And the music we sing is contemporary. We should dress to match it.[1]

Living Out Our Faith

The Reverend John Wesley, a founder of the Methodist movement, was concerned about helping his followers live in a way consistent with their faith. Realizing that people needed some help knowing the difference between right and wrong, he devised three rules known as "The General Rules of the United Societies." Wesley wrote in 1743 that he expected all those who followed him to show their desire for salvation by

1. doing no harm, avoiding evil;

2. doing good of every possible sort and, as far as possible, to all people; and

3. "attending upon all the ordinances of God." This, to Wesley, meant to use every means you could to grow closer to God, particularly taking communion, attending worship, praying, and Bible reading (adapted from The Book of Discipline, 1984, ¶67; page 51).

These three principles (do no harm, do all the good you can, do all you can to grow spiritually) are a helpful guide to us today.[2]

Life Jackets

Steve is on a camping vacation with his family. Steve's best friend Beau is with them, too. While they are staying at a lakeside camping area, Steve and Beau decide to go canoeing. Steve's younger brothers decide that they want to go canoeing, too. Steve and Beau are excellent swimmers and decide to go without wearing life preservers. When Steve's younger brothers see that the older boys are not wearing life preservers, they refuse to wear them.

Steve (*putting on a life preserver*): They're not going to wear theirs unless we wear ours. Let's go.

Beau: Wait a minute. I don't wear life jackets. I don't need one—I'm not a little kid.

Steve: I know you don't need one. Neither do I. But the little guys do. We'd be worried about them falling in the whole time we're out. Besides, my folks would get mad.

Beau: You can wear yours but I think it's dumb. I'm not going to wear one.

Steve: Come on. Put it on. I don't want to stand here all day.[3]

We Are a Forgiven People

Sometimes the things that we do are not very helpful or caring to anyone. Even if we are Christian, we can still make mistakes; our choices will not always be the best ones. This will be true even in times when we try to do right. It will be especially true in those times when we choose to do something wrong. If Christians are supposed to be such ethical people, how do we handle our own experiences of failing to do good?

We rely upon forgiveness. No other religion builds so much of its claims around the offering of a second chance. Forgiveness rescues us not only when we accept Christ but also when we do wrong. One of the most profound summaries of this viewpoint on life is found in the little letter called First John: "If we say we have no sin, we deceive ourselves, and the truth is not in us. If we confess our sins, he is faithful and just, and will forgive our sins and cleanse us from all unrighteousness" (1 John 1:8-9).

On the one hand, we human beings have to be utterly honest: We all have blown it. On the other hand, the Bible reminds us that our sin is not the bottom line. God's love is. The love that calls us to give our lives to the Lord is the same love that takes us back when we have strayed.

Three Times Three Equals a Second Chance

Talk about yielding to peer pressure. Peter was old enough to know better. But when the crunch time came and his Teacher's life was on the line, old Pete caved in. "I never knew the man. Who, me? Nah, I wasn't in his class. He wasn't my prof. You've got me confused with somebody else." He didn't just deny following Jesus, he claimed he'd never known him at all.

The next seventy-two hours must have been rough on Peter. He'd done the very thing he said he'd never do. He'd made a pledge; he'd given his word. Then he denied his Master. This was the same Peter who not long before had shouted out, "You're the Christ! The Son of God!"

When the day of Resurrection dawned and Jesus rose from the tomb, Jesus didn't wait for folks to find out about it. He went to them. He greeted women in a garden; appeared to the disciples who were hiding behind a locked door in Jerusalem; let a doubting follower touch his hands and side; and finally came to Peter.

Pete had been out fishing. Fishing was what he used to do. Perhaps Peter was looking for comfort by retreating to the past. Jesus didn't waste time. "Peter, do you love me?" he asked pointedly.

"You know I do, Lord."

"Do you really love me?"

"Yes, no question about it!" Peter was starting to get impatient when Jesus asked a third time.

"Do you love me?"

When Peter replied affirmatively once more, Jesus repeated his instructions for Peter to get out there in the world and love, love, love.

Fascinating, thought Peter, *three times I denied him, three times he forgave me. Three times three is a new beginning for me.*

And the rest, as they say, is history. You can read about it in the Book of Acts.

How Can I Thank You?

Peter could preach the gospel because he was deeply grateful for his life in Christ. Gratitude is the beginning point for making our decisions as Christians. Our entire life becomes an expression of thanks because God takes us the way we are. "We love, because he first loved us" (1 John 4:19).

Being loved first frees us to follow God with our whole hearts. Being loved first creates in us the desire to be responsible in all of our actions. Being loved first changes our character. And being loved first means that we are allowed to begin again and still be loved. There is no firmer foundation for choosing right from wrong than this love. It is ours in Jesus Christ.

Guidance System

O gracious and loving God, you know the struggles we go through trying to decide what's right and wrong. You are also aware of how we finally make our wisest choice and act upon it even when we have some uncertainties. Give us wisdom, O God, to know right from wrong and the courage to show love in all things. And forgive us when we choose wrongly. Amen.

[1] Reprint from *New Disciples*, Summer 1986, page 12. Copyright © 1986 by Graded Press.
[2] Reprint from *New Disciples*, Summer 1986, page 12. Copyright © 1986 by Graded Press.
[3] Reprint from *New Disciples*, Summer 1986, page 13. Copyright © 1986 by Graded Press.

Chapter 8

What About Heaven and Hell?

CORNERSTONE

Behind the biblical message about judgment and eternal life is the conviction that God's justice and God's love have no limits. Whether we welcome or fear that justice and love depends upon how we have chosen to live.

An Honest Struggle With Difficult Topics

"Why did God let it happen?" Sarah sounded almost angry when she posed the question. The other members of the Sunday morning youth class shrugged, looked at the floor, and kept quiet, except David.

"Maybe God knew Julie was headed for trouble somewhere down the road so he called her to heaven before it could happen. Maybe it's all for the best. I've heard some adults say that."

"Well, they're wrong!" Met, a young woman from Cambodia, was indignant. "I know God doesn't do hurtful things to people. God always helps people, just like he helped my family in all the suffering we went through."

The class members were talking through their feelings about the recent death of a very popular student who was a good friend of several students in the class. It wasn't the scheduled lesson, but they couldn't seem to concentrate on much of anything else. Mrs. Petersen, the teacher, was understanding and flexible and encouraged the young people to continue the discussion. "What do you believe happens when we die?" she inquired gently.

"We go to heaven or to—uh—to that other place, hell. Don't we?"

"I don't know. What do you think, class?"

Patty replied that in her opinion heaven and hell are figments of our human imagination, like Santa Claus and the tooth fairy.

"No, they're not! The Bible says they're real places," Allen interjected.

"Let's check it out," suggested Mrs. Petersen. "Olivia, you look up Psalm 139:8; and Jeff, you find John 14."

Olivia began to read out loud. "What's She—She—Sheol? And did I pronounce it right?"

"Yes, it's a long 'e' and a long 'o.' The Hebrew people in Old Testament times believed it was a shadowy place where people went after they died. Nothing much happened there. Everybody there was still dead. They were just together in one place."

"So where did the idea of heaven and hell come from?" asked Rosa. She added, "I think Julie is in heaven because she was a really good person. She was always kind to me."

"Jeff," Mrs, Petersen looked across the room at him. "Would you read John 14, verses 2 and 3?"

"In my Father's house are many rooms; if it were not so, would I have told you that I go to prepare a place for you? And when I go and prepare a place for you, I will come again and will take you to myself, that where I am you may be also."

Allen asked if those were Jesus' words.

"Yes, they are. He spoke them to help comfort his disciples who were growing worried about the possibility that he might die."

"When Jesus says 'house,' is it the same thing as 'heaven' ?"

"Most likely," replied Mrs. Petersen. "In other places in the New Testament, the word *heaven* is used to describe where God's people live for eternity. Just like the first disciples, it does comfort us to know Julie is in a wonderful place, doesn't it?"

"A lot! But we're still going to miss her."

"Of course you will. She was an important part of your lives, and you loved her."

Ron entered the conversation for the first time. "My folks said it was her time to go and that when it's your time, there's nothing you can do about it. I've been thinking about their statement, though; and I can't buy that."

The group members concluded that a loving God could not and would not act arbitrarily. The consensus was that God intends for each and every person to enjoy a rich, full life.

"Julie was my really good friend," offered Amy. "I know she was super neat and all, but she wasn't perfect. She said and did some things she shouldn't have. Will that mean she won't make it into heaven?"

"No way!" Jeff said emphatically. "God doesn't keep track like that. Nobody would ever make it if those were the rules."

"I've noticed that we're better at asking questions than at giving answers," observed Mrs. Petersen. "How do you feel about it?"

"A little uncomfortable," admitted Ron; "but I figure that's how it has to be with stuff as complicated as heaven and hell. Theologians have been discussing this subject for centuries. Anyhow, we won't know for certain until we die—which I hope is a long time from now. Until then I'm going to keep believing in heaven. I'm not

quite so sure what I think about that other place."

Mike, who had been quietly listening to everything, remarked, "I'm getting fidgety about this whole discussion. Why do we have to talk so much about what happens when we die. What matters is how we live right now."

Everyone nodded in agreement. Mrs. Petersen added, "What we believe about the future does shape how we act in the present. If you or I are frightened of what may happen, we will probably be insecure and troubled. On the other hand, if we are confident that God preserves life forever and that what lies ahead is beautiful beyond description, then we are free to live confidently and joyfully.

There was the sound of feet stampeding on the floor above. "It sounds like the primary class is being dismissed. Would you like to continue our discussion on heaven and hell next week?"

"Yes! Let's do!" the group members said almost in unison.

"Good. I suggest you read 1 Corinthians 15 in the meantime. Give me a call if you have any questions or if something's bothering you."

What Did Jesus Say?

According to the Synoptic Gospels (Matthew, Mark, and Luke), Jesus speaks of judgment and salvation as events that (1) begin to happen when persons encounter him and (2) are still to come in their fullness. When speaking about the future kingdom of God, Jesus assumes that life continues after death but in a different form (Mark 12:18-27). His word pictures of reward and judgment convey the message that God cares about how we live now (Mark 10:29-30; Luke 16:19-31; 23:43; Matthew 25:31-46).

The Gospel of John often presents *eternal life* as something Christians experience in their present lives (John 5:24). Likewise, this gospel repeatedly describes *judgment* as happening in the present (John 3:18-19). As the story of the raising of Lazarus makes clear (John 11:1-44), Jesus gives life now. "I am the resurrection and the life; he who believes in me, though he die, yet shall he live, and whoever lives and believes in me shall never die" (John 11:25).

But this power to grant new life continues into the future. In John 14:1-3, Jesus tells his disciples (and by implication, all who believe in him), "Let not your hearts be troubled; believe in God, believe also in me. In my Father's house are many rooms; if it were not so, would I have told you that I go to prepare a place for you? And when I go and prepare a place for you, I will come again and will take you to myself, that where I am you may be also."

Those who trust in Jesus and in God whom Jesus represents will not be abandoned in the end. They will dwell securely in the presence of the Lord. Beyond that, we can only speculate.

Resurrection of the Body

You may have wondered sometimes about the phrase in the Apostles' Creed that says "I believe . . . in the resurrection of the body." How can that be? We know that the human body decomposes after death. But people in New Testament times knew that too, in the days before refrigeration and modern funeral homes. So, what did they think about the idea of bodies coming to life? Apparently it was a puzzling idea then just as it is now. The apostle Paul recognized that confusion and saw that it was for some people an obstacle to faith.

In the First Letter to the Corinthians (15:35-58), Paul offers an analogy. He likens a seed in the ground to our earthly life from birth to death and the plant that grows from the seed to our resurrection existence. What do we make of that imagery? What is Paul trying to get across? Several things:

(1) We shouldn't expect to know in detail what resurrection life will be like. No one who looked at a seed for the first time would be able to predict what the grown plant would look like.

(2) The resurrection body will not be just the same as our earthly biological bodies. The grown plant is drastically different than the seed from which it comes. In fact, the plant is far more beautiful than the seed. So our resurrection bodies will be more glorious than our present bodies.

(3) Yet, some continuity exists between who we are now and who we will be. The seed and the plant are the same living creature but at different stages of development. We will be changed, Paul says.

However, we will still be the same people. The Christian idea of resurrection is *not* like a drop of water returning to a lake. Some element of individuality and personality will survive.

(4) The spiritual body will be different from the flesh and blood we know, but it will be a body. We are not to become disembodied spirits, mere ghosts. *Some* kind of body will be needed to express our individuality and personality.

Eternal Life Revisited

In his short novel *The Great Divorce*, C. S. Lewis describes judgment and eternal life in terms of a bus trip from hell into heaven.

This book illustrates the doctrine found all through Lewis that the innumerable choices of life inevitably condition a soul for eternity and that these choices are a perfect reflection of the will of the individual. Either a man [or woman] says to God, "Thy will be done" or God is finally forced to say to a man [or woman], "*Your* will be done."

When the bus had reached its destination within view of the glorious light and color of heaven, the passengers left it and were greeted by radiant people whose solidity made all the bus passengers so transparent they could hardly be seen. One by one the visitors were invited in, and the book consists mainly of their excuses for declining that invitation. The first was extended to the ghost of an employer by a Solid Person who had once worked for him and had committed a murder. It happened that both murderer and murdered were now residents of heaven. The ghost was astonished that he was forced to live in the pigsty of the Grey City while a murderer reached heaven. "Look at me, now," he said. "I gone straight all my life. I don't say I was a religious man and I don't say I had no faults, far from it. But I done my best all my life, see? I done my best by everyone, that's

the sort of chap I was. I never asked for anything that wasn't mine by rights. If I wanted a drink I paid for it and if I took my wages I done my job, see? . . . I'm not asking for anybody's bleeding charity." The Solid Person replied, "Then do. At once. Ask for the Bleeding Charity." Like Vertue in *The Pilgrim's Regress*, he told the Solid Person he would rather be damned than forsake his self-righteous independence and stalked off angrily on his way back to the bus. . . .

Another was the Hard-Bitten Ghost who had been everywhere and found everything a trap for tourists and a flop, even hell itself;

another well-dressed woman ghost loved her appearance more than she loved heaven, even though her finery looked ghastly in the reflected light of heaven; another was a garrulous grumbler almost at the point of becoming a grumble; another a famous artist who showed some signs of willingness to come into heaven until he discovered that his artistic reputation was unimportant there; another a wife who was willing to remain in heaven only on condition she be allowed to take up again the management of her husband . . .; another a woman whose life was selfishly taken up with mourning for a deceased son while she neglected her living daughter and husband. . . .

Of all the bus passengers only one accepted the invitation inside. He was a ghost who carried a little red lizard of lust on his shoulder and was always trying to get it to stop its ceaseless whisperings in his ear. A colossal angel came up to him and offered to destroy the lizard if he would allow it. After much tormenting persuasion the ghost desperately asked for the deed to be quickly done. The angel took the writhing, biting reptile, broke its back, and flung it on the ground. The ghost was himself left shaken and reeling as a result of the experience, but shortly he began to become solid like the other inhabitants of heaven and at the same time grew to a size little smaller than the angel. While this was taking place the lizard also took the form of a great silvery white stallion with mane and tail of gold. After flinging himself at the feet of the angel in a gesture of gratitude, the new Solid One jumped on the back of his steed and was off toward the heights of heaven like a shooting star. The very earth beneath the horse's hooves sang its joy. . . .

The Great Divorce clearly shows that cleavage between heaven and hell with eternal destiny contingent upon the soul's own choice. In the preface [Lewis] insists that the universe presents [human beings] with an unavoidable "either-or." The world is not one in which all roads lead to a center but rather one where each road shortly branches into two and those two into four and where a decision must be made at each fork. "If we insist on keeping Hell (or even earth) we shall not see Heaven: if we accept Heaven we shall not be able to retain even the smallest and most intimate souvenirs of Hell."[1]

Discussion Questions

What do you think of Lewis's imaginary description of judgment and eternal life? Does his portrayal of judgment as the result of our own choices make sense to you? Why or why not? C. S. Lewis obviously thought that our beliefs about death and resurrection make a difference in how we live. Do *your* beliefs about these matters make any difference in the way you live? How so? How can you make yourself fit for heaven? How can you make yourself *un*fit for heaven?[2]

Happy Landings

What we believe about eternal life helps shape how we live each day, how we cope with the death of a loved one or friend, and what we think and feel about our own eventual death. Belief in the fact that there is absolutely nothing in all the universe that can "separate us from the love of God in Christ Jesus our Lord" (Romans 8:39) gives us confidence to love ourselves and others. We can draw courage from the assurance that God's loving care for us never ends.

Another equally important fact is that how we live now has a determinative effect on how we will be judged whenever that time may come to pass. If we choose to live a Christian life, we have little need to feel anxiety about what the future may hold for us. The fact of the matter is that we will judge ourselves, measured by God's standards of loving and serving, of peacemaking and working for justice. Happy landings at the end of life await those whose journey follows God's way and will.

---

[1] Quoted from The Christian World of C.S. Lewis, by Clyde S. Kilby (Eerdmans, 1964); pages 44–50.

[2] Reprint from New Disciples, Spring 1987, page 19. Copyright © 1987 by Graded Press.

Chapter 9

What Is Christian About Christian Love?

CORNERSTONE

Christian love is our response to God who loved us first. We respond by loving God with our whole self and by treating others with the same care and respect we want for ourselves.

God's Love for Us

Luke 15:11-32 contains one of the most moving stories in all Scripture—but we have to be able to hear it with fresh ears. Best known as the parable of the prodigal son, it might more accurately be called the parable of the loving father. Out of the entire Bible, it gives us perhaps the best single picture of God's love.

God's love for us is undeserved. We do not *earn* it. Of course, God's love for us means that God has some expectations for us, just as truly loving parents give their kids some rules and discipline. But such parents also love their kids simply because they are their kids. In a similar way, God's love for us is where we start, not a goal out there that must be achieved.

God's love for us comes as a gift—*a terribly precious gift.*

The apostle Paul, too, recognized that God's love comes *first,* before we do anything. See what Paul says in Romans 5:6-11. God showed his love for us by allowing Jesus Christ to die for us *while we were still sinners.*

Paul assures us, as well, that God's love comes *last.* In Romans 8:31-39, Paul assures those who place their trust in Christ that nothing can ever defeat God's love for them: "For I am sure that neither death, nor life, nor angels, nor principalities, nor things present, nor things to come, nor powers, nor height, nor depth, nor anything else in all creation, will be able to separate us from the love of God in Christ Jesus our Lord" (Romans 8:38-39).

Our Response to God's Love

The love that Christians have (or should have) for other people is prompted by God's love for us. "We love, because he first loved us" (1 John 4:19). "Beloved, if God so loved us, we also ought to love one another" (1 John 4:11).

Christian love looks to the neighbor's need. Christian love finds ways to be a neighbor to those in need. Do you recall the parable of the good Samaritan (Luke 10:29-37)? That's what Christian love is like! That's what Christians should be doing! Christians are supposed to be the kind of people who fulfill Jesus' new commandment to love (see John 13:34-35; 15:12-17).

The *depth* of Christian love is measured against the plumb line of divine love. God loves us graciously, not because of our merit. To a lesser degree, we can model that love by giving ourselves for others.

The *range* or *scope* of Christian love is universal. No one is excluded because he or she is not one of "us." Christian love reaches out to all people.

The Two Great Commandments

"But when the Pharisees heard that he had silenced the Sadducees, they came together. And one of them, a lawyer, asked him a question, to test him. 'Teacher, which is the great commandment in the law?' And he said to him, 'You shall love the Lord your God with all your heart, and with all your soul, and with all your mind. This is the great and first commandment. And a second is like it, You shall love your neighbor as yourself. On these two commandments depend all the law and the prophets'" (Matthew 22:34-40).

Jesus brought together two basic commandments from the Old Testament. Deuteronomy 6:4-5, called the Shema (meaning "hear"), reminded the people that God expected their complete devotion, their whole being. Leviticus 19:18 made plain that God also expected the people of Israel to show love for their neighbors. In a nutshell, that is what Christian love is about: (1) loving God with heart and soul and mind and (2) treating one's neighbor with care and respect (implied, of course, is that one's *own* self is worthy of care and respect).

Fill in the Blanks

God says, "I will love you no matter whether you're good, beautiful, get high grades, or eat your spinach." His love is __ __-__ __ __ __ __ __ __ __-__ __. We've done nothing to earn it. It's __ __ __ __. Since it's a gift, there is no cost. All we have to do is __ __ __ __ __ __ __ it. No one is excluded from the offer: young or old, female or male, rich, poor, or in-between. God's love is __ __ __ __ __ __-__ __ __ and is for all creation. There are also no time limits on love. Love never ends. It's _____.

God's love _____ us when we commit a sin or fail to live according to his __ __ __ __. We are accepted as we are, but we are expected to __ __ __ __ in love and maturity. Love has different aspects. __ __ __ __ refers to romantic, desiring love. _____-__ __ refers to brotherly or sisterly love. When love is totally self-giving and expects no return whatsoever, the Greek word is __ __ __ __ __ __. We should not confuse giving love with ease and complacency. Woven together with love are __ __ __ __ __ __ __ __ and _____. When we are _____ that God loves us, we want to show it by __ __ __ __ __ __ __-_____ to others and by _____-_____ the world.

Words to Choose

(Each word is used once.)

justice	free
eternal	agape
grow	receive
assured	inclusive
Eros	will
witnessing	forgives
unconditional	Phileo
serving	discipline

A Paraphrase of 1 Corinthians 13

If I can speak eloquently but do not love, I am like a noisy rock band playing off key. If I possess a photographic memory and have a computer for a brain and if I have faith strong enough to change the shape of the world but don't love people, I'm nothing but a big zero. Even if I were to give away everything I own—money, bicycle, car, tapes, records, clothes—without love, I'm a loser.

Love is patient and kind. Love doesn't get jealous or act like a big shot. Love never says, "Do it my way or forget it." It doesn't hold grudges or act resentfully. It hardly even notices when someone tries to hurt it. Love never enjoys it when others get into trouble but celebrates when everyone succeeds. Love can put up with anything and still keep on loving.

It never ends. All the bright ideas the human race has ever devised will one day disappear.

When I was a little kid, I acted like a little kid. Now that I'm maturing, I'm trying to quit acting childishly. I don't pretend to understand all these mysteries about life, the future, and God. But I've figured out this much: There are three enduring qualities—faith, hope, and love. And love is tops! So go for it!

Real Love

Frances was fifteen when her brother was killed in a motorcycle accident. The night before he died, she had a date with Evan, her boy friend. After a movie, they had sat on the wall of a vacant lot down the street from her house. It was that night that Evan told her he loved her more than he had ever loved any other girl. Frances had a hard time going to sleep. Evan loved her!

And then came the next morning, the terrible morning she would never forget. Her brother, two years older, left home early and rode his motorcycle to school. It was over in an instant. The car speeded up to make it through the yellow light. Minutes later, the police were at the front door, breaking the news. A little while later and Frances would have been on the school bus, and would have missed them.

Evan heard about the accident at lunchtime. He felt sick, as he remembered that he had never really liked Frances' brother. He wondered how she must feel. Evan wondered what he could possibly say to her. How could he pretend to be sorry, when she knew he didn't like her brother anyway? What if she cried? He supposed she would. Better to wait a while, to think of something right or clever to say.

But Evan never did think of anything to say. He avoided Frances' house, and didn't call her.

Frances couldn't believe it. Only the night before, Evan had told her he loved her more than anyone. Why didn't he stop by, or

at least call? It would have been so good to see him, to hear his voice. Had he somehow missed the news? That was impossible. It had been on the radio all day; everyone at school was talking about it. Night came, the worst night of her life, as she and her parents cried together as if their hearts were broken.

Evan never called. He could never think of anything to say.

Evan said he *loved* Frances. He probably thought he meant what he said. But did he really love her? Not if loving means choosing to care for another person. If Evan really cared for her, wouldn't he have put her above his own feelings?

Jesus, on the other hand, knew that love is not really a feeling at all, but a way of living. It is *how you act*, not how fast your heart beats.[1]

Drawing Big Enough Circles

God's Word repeatedly reminds us that when it comes to love, we often are stingy. We are to love God with ALL our heart and with ALL our soul and with ALL our might (Deuteronomy 6:5). God has extravagantly given us his love. We are to respond by loving with all our being.

Love is not simply a pleasant emotion, a warm feeling inside. Love is a way of life. It is commitment, compassion, and caring. Love extends beyond the circle of our immediate family, friends, and acquaintances. It is to be offered even to those with whom we disagree, who come from political or economic systems different from ours, whose religious beliefs are widely divergent.

Christian love ultimately draws its circle so big that it includes persons and nations labeled enemies. "You have heard that it was said, 'You shall love your neighbor and hate your enemy.' But I say to you, 'Love your enemies and pray for those who persecute you. . . . For if you love those who love you, what reward have you? Do not even the tax collectors do the same?'" (Matthew 5:43-46).

One of the unique dimensions of Christian love is that it expects nothing in return. It is given freely to all persons, regardless of age, sex, status, outward appearance. It may not be easy to love one's enemies, but in Christ it is possible.

Outcasts

Unfortunately, the attitude Snoopy ran into is not limited to cartoon strips. Real people reject other people—treat them as outcasts—all too often. Sometimes the "reasons" for finding others undesirable are obvious, sometimes subtle. Sometimes the way persons are rejected is obvious, other times subtle. But no matter how it is expressed, it is painful to the one who learns he or she is unwelcome.

Who are some of the people who are viewed as social outcasts today (in your school or your community)?

What are some ways that persons are made to feel unwelcome, as unworthy?

How do you think Christians should behave toward persons who are considered undesirable?[2]

---

[1] Reprinted from A *Faith for Teenagers* by John Kater, available from Cowley Publications, 980 Memorial Drive, Cambridge, MA 02138 (copyright 1987); pages 70–73.
[2] Reprint from *New Disciples*, Spring 1987, page 48. Copyright © 1987 by Graded Press.

Chapter 10

Are Science and Faith Compatible?

CORNERSTONE

Science, properly understood, is neither a threat to Christian faith nor a substitute for it.

Science-Faith Chart

Science	Faith
Looks at the visible, observable universe	Is open to things not seen
Employs reason and logic	Involves the whole person (heart, mind, soul)
Attempts to be objective	Leaves room for subjectivity
Conducts experiments	Puts a premium on trust
Deals in quantitative terms	Focuses on qualitative matters
Hypotheses, theorems, formulas	Hymns, stories, prayer
Tries to avoid value judgments	Is passionate about values: peace, justice, equality
Tries to explain everything it can in natural terms	Enjoys leaving room for mystery, wonder, and awe
Subject of its study is always a preliminary concern	Nature of subject is ultimate concern

From Win-Lose to Win-Win

Straw creatures are fun to decorate for Halloween when we call them scarecrows. But sometimes in intellectual discussions people concoct false images of an opposing view simply so they may attack it and easily reveal its inadequacies. In the ongoing dialogue between science and faith, both sides have frequently used this approach. Science has labeled faith as nothing more than wishful thinking, the product of a hyperactive human imagination. Faith has sometimes accused science of playing God, of pridefully thinking that nothing but science matters.

Whenever faith or science becomes expressed narrowly, implying that it alone possesses truth, conflict will follow. If science stays within the parameters of its inquiry, if it accepts the limits of its scope, and if faith comprehends its central purpose, coexistence between the two is possible.

Science asks the questions, What? How? When? For example, it asks, What happened when the universe was created. It postulates a Big Bang Theory to explain the fact that the universe is expanding at a rapid rate. Science seeks to determine what mechanical forces and elements worked together to bring forth life. It asks, When did life begin?

On the other hand, faith asks, Who brought this marvelous creation into existence? And why? For what purpose did an Ultimate Being fashion this universe and bring forth life on at least one small planet?

Sometimes science and faith have behaved badly toward each other. The supporters of a scientific viewpoint have been afraid that individuals who define faith in their own narrow terms will foist their doctrines on others. That has happened. Cults are classic examples. And when science implies that faith is nothing more than magic and hocus-pocus, faith can become a bit defensive.

The conflict has centered recently around the issues of evolutionary theory and creationism. One of the scientific explanations is that creation is an unfolding process. Over a period of centuries (even millennia), life changes, develops, evolves. Biblical literalists find this idea antithetical to their belief that God brought the world and its inhabitants into being in six twenty-four-hour days, completing the task perfectly, no changes ever needed.

The Bible, however, was not written as a scientific treatise. Chapters One and Two of Genesis poetically offer two explanations of Creation. But both have as their primary purpose the proclamation of whose power and creativity brought the world into being. "In the beginning God created . . . God was moving . . . God said . . . God saw . . . God separated . . . God called . . . God made . . . God set . . . God rested . . ." The purpose obviously is to answer the question, Who?

A no-win situation exists when narrow-minded persons on either side argue about science and faith. The best wisdom available clearly suggests that both viewpoints have validity within the scope of their respective disciplines. Both pursue truth. Both seek to make sense out of life.

Jesus said, "You will know the truth, and the truth will make you free" (John 8:32). No matter what the specific tools a person uses, the kind of vocabulary employed, or the particular techniques developed, when truth is discovered, it has freeing power. And that is a win-win situation.

Comparing Apples and Oranges

You've heard the saying, "Don't try to compare apples and oranges." An apple has a distinctive shape, is crisp and crunchy with a skin you can eat. Oranges were honored with a color named for them, are juicy, have segments, and have a peel that is not particularly edible. Apples and oranges are quite different from each other, yet both are tasty and nutritious. They look appetizing next to each other in a fruit salad. It does little good to criticize an apple for not being an orange or vice versa. We should rejoice when apples are true to their "appleness" and be glad when oranges are the best oranges they can possibly be.

The same thing holds for science and faith. Rather than complain that one isn't able to explain everything under the sun (or beyond the sun), we should be content with faith being faith and science being science. Science and faith are not in competition; they are complementary endeavors in the search for truth. Neither field of inquiry can claim a corner on the truth market. When both employ their own methods with integrity and humility, a harmonious relationship is possible.

Scientists can be persons of faith. And persons of faith are able to embrace the truths of scientific discovery.

Chapter 11

Are Science and Faith Compatible? (continued)

CORNERSTONE
The newest discoveries of science point to the essential mystery of life on earth and can lead us toward a deeper appreciation of God as Creator.

What In the World . . .?

The world is chock full of truly astounding things—for those who have "eyes to see" and "ears to hear." Even "ordinary" things are marvelously intricate. Can you identify the objects in the photos on these two pages?

Here are a few clues:

1. It flies through the air with the greatest of ease—but needs no trapeze.

2. To find one, look under the sea—or in the dictionary under "C."

3. It has gills, but it is not a fish. And it is not too big.

4. A _____ by any other name is still a _____.

You can check your guesses against the answers at the bottom of page 67.

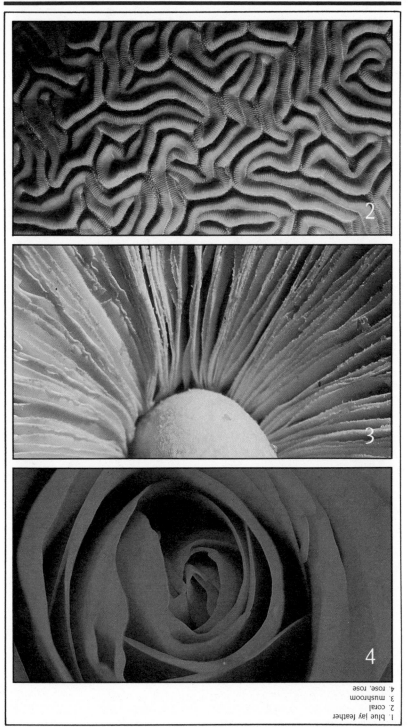

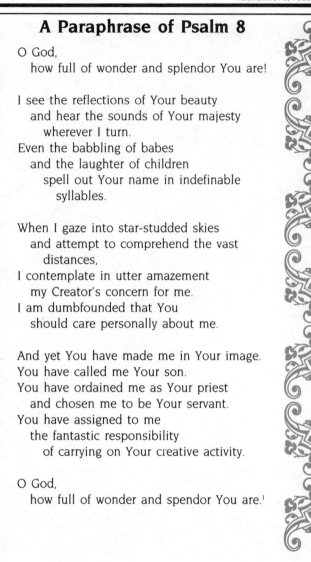

A Paraphrase of Psalm 8

O God,
    how full of wonder and splendor You are!

I see the reflections of Your beauty
    and hear the sounds of Your majesty
        wherever I turn.
Even the babbling of babes
    and the laughter of children
        spell out Your name in indefinable
        syllables.

When I gaze into star-studded skies
    and attempt to comprehend the vast
        distances,
I contemplate in utter amazement
    my Creator's concern for me.
I am dumbfounded that You
    should care personally about me.

And yet You have made me in Your image.
You have called me Your son.
You have ordained me as Your priest
    and chosen me to be Your servant.
You have assigned to me
    the fantastic responsibility
        of carrying on Your creative activity.

O God,
    how full of wonder and spendor You are.[1]

Interview With Madeleine L'Engle

Madeleine L'Engle is the author of thirty-four books, including the New-berry Award-Winning A Wrinkle in Time. In the course of her long and distinguished career as a writer, she has emerged as an insightful and respected lay theologian. The relation of science and faith have long been of particular interest to her. Following is a transcript of a phone interview conducted with Madeleine L'Engle.

Foundations: "How do you think your writing would be different if you weren't a Christian?"

Madeleine L'Engle: "I don't know because I am a Christian because of my writing and not the other way around."

Foundations: "Oh, would you say a little more about that? How do you think that you became a Christian because of your writing?"

Madeleine L'Engle: "Well, I was born of parents who were Episcopalians whose parents were Episcopalians whose parents were Episcopalians and I grew up in a Christian household where I more or less took it for granted, as most of us do who grow up that way. I spent 6 years in Anglican boarding schools which is enough to turn one against the establishment. And I left it—quite obviously—I mean, there are a lot of things wrong with the establishment and when we're young, we're very intolerant. And so since the establishment was lousy, I quit. I didn't quit God, I just quit the establishment. But by then I was already firmly involved in writing and I married and had children and we were living up here in the country and going to this congregational church which was the only church in the village, really, and I was asking a lot of questions about how one believes in God and how one believes in Jesus. And I was given German theologians to read and I read them and shook my head and thought, no, if I have to believe all of this garbage, Christianity's not for me. And then I discovered Einstein's theories of relativity and higher math and the new insights into particle physics and quantum mechanics and I found my theology. And Einstein says anyone who is not lost in rapturous awe and joy at the power of the mind behind the universe is as good as a burnt-out candle. I thought, yes, good, that's good theology."

Foundations: "And so many people see a conflict between science and religion that you obviously don't."

Madeleine L'Engle: "How can there be a conflict? I don't understand how there can be a conflict—anything science shows us simply reveals more of the glory of God and a far more glorious universe than we ever believed and its wonderful. It is a totally interrelated universe that is in unity and anything—anybody—does affect the whole of it. I then wrote my eleventh book, A *Wrinkle in Time*, and that was to me a theological enterprise. I was writing about a universe in which I could believe in the love of God who really counts the hairs upon our heads and the fall of every sparrow. And as I wrote the book—when I write I'd listen, and I learned and that was the moment at which I realized that my writing was my vocation and not just a career."[2]

Both Science and Faith Sometimes Go Barefoot

Newtonian physics assumed that as measurements became more precise and scientific instruments more refined, all the unknowns in the universe could eventually be explained. It would simply be a matter of time until the tools and techniques were perfected. But science after Einstein's theories has never been the same.

The more scientists have discovered, the more they find there is yet to know. Surprises abound in nature and throughout the universe. As more is understood about the workings of things visible, more mysteries are uncovered than anyone ever dreamt. New forces have been observed in the far reaches of space. Molecular structure has been found to have an occasional "rebellious streak" and to behave in rather unpredictable ways.

There is mystery in an exploding super nova and in a tiny ice crystal, in massive storms on the sun's surface and in a dandelion gone to seed, in butterflies and buttercups and snowflakes. The response of the scientist is to probe and explore ever more deeply. The response of the person of faith is to give thanks, to offer praise, to feel reverent.

When Moses saw the burning bush in the mountain wilderness (Exodus 3:1-6), a bush that was in flame but not consumed by the fire, he was awe-struck. He heard God calling him to lead the people out of slavery. In wonder at the marvelous mystery, Moses took off his shoes because it was holy ground upon which he stood.

The entire universe is "holy ground" that we must respect. Every part of it is crammed with surprises and miracles and mysteries. It awaits discovery by the inquiring mind, the perceptive eye, and the receptive spirit of persons both in science and of faith.

Post-modern science cannot prove God's existence. But it can and does show us genuine mystery in nature—and that may point beyond itself to the ultimate, transcendent mystery that is God. Unlike the outdated mechanical picture of reality, post-modern science leaves plenty of room for a plausible belief in God the Creator and Sustainer of the world.

In Romans 11:33-36, the apostle Paul seems strikingly relevant to our age: "O depth of wealth, wisdom, and knowledge in God! How unsearchable his judgements, how untraceable his ways! Who knows the mind of the Lord? Who has been his counsellor? Who has ever made a gift to him, to receive a gift in return? Source, Guide, and Goal of all that is—to him be glory for ever! Amen."[3]

Humans as Part of Creation

There is in all of us a need to be part of something. We all want to know that we belong. The thought that we do not can be very painful.

Genesis 1:27 tells us that humans were part of God's created order. Humans were not an afterthought thrown in to make the equation come out correctly. Rather, humans were an integral part of the process.

However, lest we take undue pride in our place, let us remember that we are *part* of all that was created. We are not *all* that was created.

Therefore, we have a relationship with all that exists on the earth. Other parts of creation are not alien to us or evil. We have a common link to all that exists on our planet; like us, everything is part of the created order.

We do not have to worry that creation just happened. It was a thought out process, and we are an integral part of that order.[4]

To Have Dominion

There is an old saying, "a place for everything, and everything in its place." The idea behind this is one of order—a given purpose and place for each item.

The Genesis creation story tells of a given place and role for all its parts. The sun, moon, and the stars each have a place and a purpose (Genesis 1:16-18). The birds, sea monsters, and every living creature had a place and purpose (Genesis 1:20-22).

Humankind was also given a very particular role, expressed in Genesis and in Psalm 8. The psalmist, in this hymn of praise to God, tells how we have been given a place just below the angels, but for the specific reason of "dominion over the works of thy hands" (Psalm 8:6).

This place in the order created by God out of goodness carries an honor and a responsibility. It gives us a very definite role. It is a role granted by God: We are to rule the earth under God's ultimate rule. The biblical idea is that we fill in for God by keeping the order the way God intended it to be.

It is important to remember that the power and authority that humans are to use has been given by God. We did not grasp the power in rebellion or have to demand our place. God chose to *give* us power and authority as an honor and a responsibility. Like the psalmist, there is no other response for us, but "O Lord, our Lord, how majestic is thy name in all the earth (Psalm 8:9).[5]

[1] From *Psalms/Now* (Leslie F. Brandt) Copyright © 1973 Concordia Publishing House. Used by permission.

[2] Reprint from *New Disciples Media Kit*, Summer 1987. Copyright © 1987 by Graded Press. (transcript of a telephone interview between noted authors Nancy Veglahn and Madeleine L'Engle)

[3] From *The New English Bible* © The Delegates of the Oxford University Press and The Syndics of the Cambridge University Press, 1961, 1970. Reprinted by permission.

[4] Reprint from *New Disciples*, Fall 1987, page 3. Copyright © 1987 by Graded Press.

[5] Reprint from *New Disciples*, Fall 1987, page 7. Copyright © 1987 by Graded Press.

Chapter 12

Why Be a Part of the Church?

CORNERSTONE
Through the church we can find an identity for our-selves: We are members of the people of God.

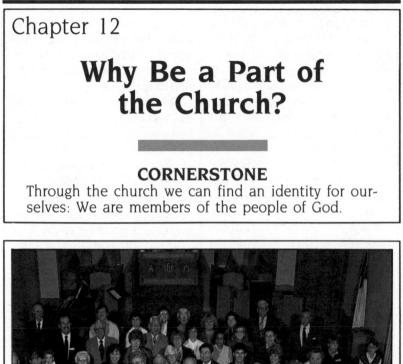

Our Family Album

Reminiscing is fun. You pull out the dusty family album and start thumbing through it. Photographs trigger memories that bubble up from your past. They may be a mixture of joyful and painful rec-ollections, attended by laughter or by tears.

If the church had a family album, it would include snapshots of events in Jerusalem on the day of Pentecost (fifty days after Pass-over or the resurrection of Jesus). Acts 2 tells the story. There would be pictures of people from different countries, talking at the same time and understanding every word; Peter pounding on the pulpit as he preached; a sort of an aurora borealis of fire hovering above; and messed up hair from the mighty wind that rushed through. There would be scenes of Paul traveling across the Mediterranean Sea and standing beside all the different churches he started. There would also be scenes of Timothy and Titus, of Mary and Martha, of Stephen, of Priscilla, and of a host of other people at work and at play. Suffering and rejoicing would appear on the pages.

This family album would of necessity be multivolumed; and each book would be thick because priests and prophets, scholars and reformers, mystics and theologians, children and youth, famous and humble folks, would be arm in arm.

The truly wonderful thing about this album is that there are empty pages for the present and future church family to fill. Perhaps there will be more pages than the total already completed. Might there be a few candid shots of you?

A People and Its Story

Any human family consists of people of all ages, some of whom live nearby while others have moved across the country or the world. A family also includes those who have died and those who have not yet been born. Every family has a collection of stories, special times and places, that belong to its members alone. Those memories are told and passed on whenever families get together. Sometimes they last for many years and spread thousands of miles, as people move from place to place.

It was a hot August morning when Philip began putting his gear together. The most important thing was his fishing rod. It had belonged to his grandfather, and some of Philip's earliest memories were of going fishing with him. Even when he was so small he had to run to keep up, his grandfather would stop by and they would go off together. Those outings were one of the things Philip had missed most since his grandfather died. Now he was old enough to enjoy going alone, but it wasn't the same.

Philip's brother Charlie was five years younger. At nine, he was too young to remember Grandad. Sometimes Charlie stared at the photograph in the dining room, but although he tried and tried, there was no memory of him, only that picture.

For a long time, Charlie had been trying to talk his brother into taking him fishing. This morning was no different. "Come on, Phil," he began as Philip was packing his lunch for a day on the river. "Please let me come with you."

"You'll make too much noise," Philip replied, as he always did.

"No I won't; I promise I won't make a sound."

Philip looked down at his brother, so eager for this expedition. For the first time, he decided to give it a try. . . .

The day passed as slowly as August days always seemed to go. Charlie was fascinated by how much Philip knew about fishing in this river. Philip showed his brother how to bait his hook, how to cast the line so that it missed the tangle of roots by the edge of the shoreline, and—when at last there was a twitching on Charlie's line—how to set the hook and reel in the fish. . . . As they walked home in the late afternoon, he asked Phil, "How did you ever learn so much about fishing?"

"That's easy," Phil answered. "Grandad taught me all about it. . . .

And then Philip began to talk about his grandfather: how much he had liked to be with him, what a good story-teller he was, how his grandfather used to take him on walks in the woods when the leaves were falling and build huge piles for Phil to jump in. Charlie was intrigued. He had never known this man Phil remembered, but when they got home he looked again, long and hard, at the photograph in the dining room. It seemed as if the old man was no longer a stranger. . .

The day he went fishing with his older brother, Charlie learned something very important about being a member of his family. . . . He learned new skills, which had been in the family a long time and now belonged to him. He learned something about where he had come from, and the people who had belonged to his family before he was born. . . . From that day on, whenever Charlie would go fishing, he would remember the stories of his grandfather and what his brother had taught him. Fishing would not be just another pastime; it would be a way of remembering some of his family's most prized memories. Rosalie, their little sister, was only five now, but already Charlie could imagine himself taking her fishing someday. . . .

You could say that Christians are also a family. The community of Christians is bound together by memories, by the things they have in common, by their love of one another, and by all the hopes they share which have not yet come true. . . . There are many things we share. For one thing, we tell the same stories. If you travel five thousand miles and go to church, you will hear the same tales about Jesus and his companions that you heard at home. Christians also celebrate the same things. We all participate in holidays like Christmas and Easter. Even though one part of the family may have different customs for celebrating, the holidays are the same. . . . For twenty centuries, Christians have been baptizing their children and sharing bread and wine together.

You might say, too, that Christians are members of a community. Communities also share memories and stories, share special actions and gestures. Have you ever gone to a new school? Part of learning to feel at home and *belonging* comes from hearing stories about a particular teacher or a legendary football game, picking up the slang that identifies you as a student of that school, wearing a school jacket or T-shirt. When you begin to know and understand these memories and rituals, you have become part of the community. Years later, the words of a football cheer or your school's song will remind you of what it was like to be there.

We have ancestors we share: we are all the spiritual descendants of Abraham and Sarah. Christians trace their ancestry through the people of Israel to the time of Jesus, and then through the company of Jesus' friends who have carried on his story through two thousand years. This Christian people is the *church*.

Christians are a people who have tried for as long as they have been in existence to understand what it means to be part of this family, this community. They have wondered about God, and the universe. They have tried to figure out how human beings ought to live, what is the purpose of their lives, how to find love and what to do about the fact that we all die sooner or later. Sometimes they have tried to find ways of avoiding those questions, but the questions keep coming back.[1]

Looking Backward to Go Forward

Learning to drive is a fascinating adventure. The major challenge is to coordinate all the gadgets: accelerator, clutch, brake, gearshift lever, and steering wheel; to watch the various gauges; to keep your eyes on the road ahead; AND occasionally to check the rearview mirrors. It's important to see where you're going, but it's also crucial to know where you've been and what's going on behind.

Learning to drive is an apt analogy for life in the church. Some folks spend so much time rearview mirror gazing that they crash into rather obvious hazards on the highway, or else they simply stop so their backward looking can continue uninterrupted. Others speed ahead unmindful that anyone is behind them, unaware that to get somewhere means you've come from someplace. Our destination is connected to the location of our origins.

A healthy balance is needed. The church is a forward looking, moving institution; but it has a rich and informative past. Frequent glances toward our history as the people of God give us assurance and guidance for the faith journey ahead.

The following examples are a small sample of significant biblical persons whose struggles and victories offer us insight into our search for meaning and identity.

(1) ABRAHAM AND SARAH: They obeyed and followed God's commands even though they didn't fully understand. They laughed at God's promise of the birth of a son in their old age, but they kept going and made the best of a joyfully difficult life.

(2) ISAAC AND REBEKAH: They were parents of children who were less than ideal, who were given to extreme fits of jealousy, showed favoritism, argued, schemed, plotted, and deceived. Yet that family became a source of blessing for the nation and for generations to come.

(3) JACOB AND RACHEL: Their family life was stressful, to say the least. They literally wrestled with what it meant to be part of the people of God. They found the strength to be parents of children who were later the leaders of the tribes of Israel.

(4) HOSEA AND GOMER: A husband and wife in the eighth century B.C., they experienced a painful marriage and were separated. Following a reconciliation, their personal lives served as models for God's people, calling the community of faith to renewed commitment.

(5) MARY AND JOSEPH: This couple were entrusted with raising a "gifted" child, a task that must have been rather frightening at times. They had to flee for their lives, lost their son in the Temple, and were told of emotional pain that would one day occur. Small wonder Mary pondered all this in her heart.

(6) LOIS, EUNICE, AND TIMOTHY: A grandmother, mother, and son who expressed sincere faith in God, who shared love in their home, and by their witness were blessings to the early church.

Great leaders, effective teachers, eloquent prophets, energetic missionaries and preachers, sensitive poets and skilled musicians, brave martyrs—these and countless others have brought the church to where it is today. Like us, these persons from our past made mistakes—the Bible, for example, reads in places like a juicy soap opera or a racy romance. Like us, these people were human beings trying their best to serve God. That's why it's helpful to look in the rearview mirror once in a while to catch sight of where the people of God have come from. Doing so will help us as we move forward in our quest to become our best.

Stained-Glass Definitions

(1) **Baptism:** The sacrament using water; it serves as the entry point into the church.

(2) **catholic:** With a small "c"; it refers to the universal church.

(3) **Catholic:** With a capital "C"; it refers specifically to the Roman Catholic Church.

(4) **Diakonia:** Serving God in concrete ways; a dominant theme in the Letter of James.

(5) **Disciple:** One who follows the teachings of a master; one who is intent on becoming a more effective follower of Jesus Christ.

(6) **Ecclesia:** Greek for *church* or *congregation*; it literally means "those who are called out."

(7) **Ecumenical:** Worldwide or universal; it particularly refers to church unity and cooperation.

(8) **Eucharist:** The sacrament of the Lord's Supper (Communion) begun by Jesus with his disciples in the upper room (read 1 Corinthians 11:23-26).

(9) **Evangelism:** The sharing of the gospel of Jesus Christ through personal example, preaching, teaching, or service.

(10) **Gathered Church:** The people of God as they gather for worship, study, and fellowship.

(11) **Koinonia:** Based on the Greek word for *common*; it means to have a common bond with other Christians, to be in partnership and in fellowship.

(12) **Laity:** Laypersons in the church as distinguished from the ordained clergy.

(13) **Liturgy:** Literally "the work of the people of God" in worship. The ritual or form of our worship together.

(14) **Pentecost:** Traditionally called the birthday of the Christian church; fifty days after Passover and the resurrection of Jesus.

(15) **Sacrament:** Two rites (in Protestantism) of baptism and Communion practiced by Jesus as a means of conveying God's grace.

(16) **Scattered Church:** The people of God sent forth to be in mission to the world—at school, home, work, everywhere.

[1] From A *Faith for Teenagers*, by John Kater, available from Cowley Publications, 980 Memorial Drive, Cambridge, MA 02138 (copyright 1987); pages 17–23.

Chapter 13

Why Be a Part of the Church? (continued)

CORNERSTONE
In the church—the *body of Christ* and the *fellowship of believers*—we can find others with whom to share our joys, our sorrows, and our eagerness to help people in need.

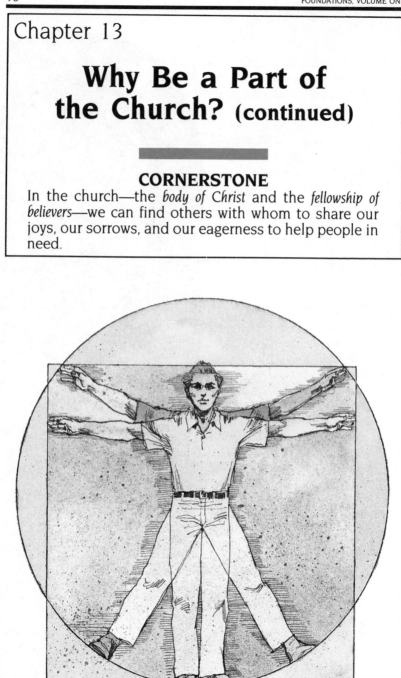

The Body of Christ

"For as in one body we have many members, and all the members do not have the same function, so we, though many, are one body in Christ, and individually members one of another. Having gifts that differ according to the grace given to us, let us use them" (Romans 12:4-6a).

"Speaking the truth in love, we are to grow up in every way into him who is the head, into Christ, from whom the whole body, joined and knit together by every joint with which it is supplied, when each part is working properly, makes bodily growth and up-builds itself in love" (Ephesians 4:15-16).

In the New Testament, the church is described as the *body of Christ*. What does that mean?

It means, first of all, that the church is characterized by a profound unity. Just like a human body with many organs, each of which is necessary for the health and well-being of the person, the church includes many members, each with different talents and tasks that serve a common purpose. When one part hurts, the whole body feels the pain. (Remember what it feels like to have a finger smashed in a car door?) When part of the church rejoices, the whole church joins in the glory. For service, for support, and for celebration—the church is a body of interdependent believers.

But this is not just *any* body. It is the body of Christ. The New Testament describes Christ as the head of the church. That means that its members share a common loyalty and serve a common purpose. We are intimately connected to Christ.

Fellowship of Believers

Have you ever joined a club or organization? Scouts? a sports team? a school club? a youth group? To become a member of that group you have to meet the requirements for admission.

There is a sense in which the church is like this too. At some point in our life we choose or affirm Christ as our Savior. That confession has an effect not only on us as individual persons; it also immediately "inducts" us into the church.

As a result, there is no such thing as a lone Christian. To accept Christ means to enter into the fellowship of all believers.

Christ is the basis of the fellowship that Christians have in common. In fact, the word in the New Testament for "fellowship"—*koinonia*—is based on the word *common*. You are certainly aware of how many different kinds of people are part of your own congregation: young, old, large, small, houseparents, secretaries, teachers, doctors, the unemployed, students. You are especially blessed if your congregation includes people of various races, for each background brings a richness to the way that faith is lived. But for all the differences, Christians have Christ in common.

Koinonia also means "partners participating." To have fellowship in Christ, the church therefore is involved with itself, with each member throughout the wold. The apostle Paul spoke to one of the first churches this way: "thankful for your partnership in the gospel from the first day until now" (Philippians 1:5). In prison at the time he wrote this letter, Paul reminded this young congregation that they shared life with him in spite of his circumstances.

Paul used the same koinonia to remind his Philippian readers of what their common bond, Christ, did for them. We participate together in the One who gave himself for us, all the way to death. Paul strove for this way of life and wanted the others to do the same: "that I may . . . share his sufferings, becoming like him in his death" (Philippians 3:10).

As a result, koinonia calls us to take care of one another as Christians. There are many ways in which the members of a church family can help one another and so share fellowship: visiting shut-ins, doing yard work for housebound members, providing a pool for babysitting, serving at a church dinner, stuffing envelopes in the church office, and so forth. Adults are not always alert enough to allow teenagers the opportunity to participate. If you make the effort to offer your time and to accept the responsibility, you can help adults grow in *their* understanding of koinonia!

Hope for Hypocrites and Other Normal People

The church is filled with beautiful people and nerds, side by side; with incredibly courageous folks and wimps; the rich and famous next to the down and out; those who have failed or are in grief sitting beside those who have succeeded and are rejoicing; some who are totally exhausted and some who are bubbling over with energy—all together. And each one needs all the others, both on the receiving and on the giving end.

A transformation occurs when this collection of interesting individuals is joined into the fellowship of believers. Their individual strands are woven into a wonderfully beautiful tapestry. They become integral parts of the body of Christ. The personal imperfections remain. There are still zits and ingrown toenails. But there is something far greater: The Spirit of God gives glory to the church. Paul writes that Christ loved the church "that he might present the church to himself in splendor, without spot or wrinkle or any such thing, that she might be holy and without blemish" (Ephesians 5:27).

Who wouldn't want to belong to an organization like this?